AN INTRODUCTION TO
EGYPTOLOGY

AN INTRODUCTION TO
EGYPTOLOGY

JAMES PUTNAM

CHARTWELL
BOOKS, INC.

A QUANTUM BOOK

Published by Chartwell Books
A Division of Book Sales Inc.
114 Northfield Avenue
Edison, New Jersey 08837
USA

Copyright ©MCMXC
Quintet Publishing Ltd

This edition printed 2002

ISBN 0-7858-1606-2

QUMEGY

This book is produced by
Quantum Publishing Ltd
6 Blundell Street
London N7 9BH

Printed in Singapore by
Star Standard Industries (Pte) Ltd

CONTENTS

CHAPTER ONE

The
STUDY
of
ANCIENT
EGYPT

ABOVE: *Jean François
Champollion (1790–1832)
– the 'Father of
Egyptology' and the
decipherer of hieroglyphs.*

Although knowledge of the civilization and language of the Ancient Egyptians was lost for many centuries, their impressive monuments remained a source of amazement and curiosity to all Europeans who travelled to Egypt. Greek and Roman writers recorded their journeys and throughout medieval times pilgrims passed through Egypt on their way to the Holy Land. By the eighteenth century many travellers had published accounts of their journeys which often included detailed illustrations of the amazing things they saw. These images of Ancient Egypt appeared alien to Europeans, who were more familiar with their classical heritage. The languages of this heritage, Greek and Latin, had been maintained and its art and architecture had enjoyed fashionable revivals. The mysterious hieroglyphs, weird animal-headed gods and exotic costumes of Ancient Egypt appeared to Europeans of the past, as they do to us nowadays, very strange indeed.

The first major study of Ancient Egyptian civilization was undertaken by a group of French scholars who accompanied Napoleon's Egyptian campaign in 1798. They took with them artists to record what they saw and they eventually published a whole series of beautifully illustrated volumes called the *Description de L'Egypte*. At this time the French Army discovered a stone at a place called Rosetta which had the same text inscribed on it in Greek, hieroglyphics and another Egyptian text called Demotic. This inscription was to provide the Frenchman, Champollion, with the key to deciphering the hieroglyphs after 20 years of dedicated study. The decipherment of the script between 1822 and 1824 and the publication of the multi-volume work, the *Description de L'Egypte 1809–30,* mark the beginning of Egyptology as a separate subject.

After his success with understanding the hieroglyphs, Champollion mounted a joint expedition with an Italian called Rosellini, to record the Egyptian monuments in detail. As a result they each produced beautifully illustrated publications which, together with the *Description de L'Egypte,* did much to popularize Ancient Egypt throughout Europe. They also inspired more travellers and merchants to visit Egypt, attracted not only by eager curiosity but by the opportunity to return with antiquities which were becoming valuable. We should not forget that at this time travel to Egypt was lengthy and hazardous,

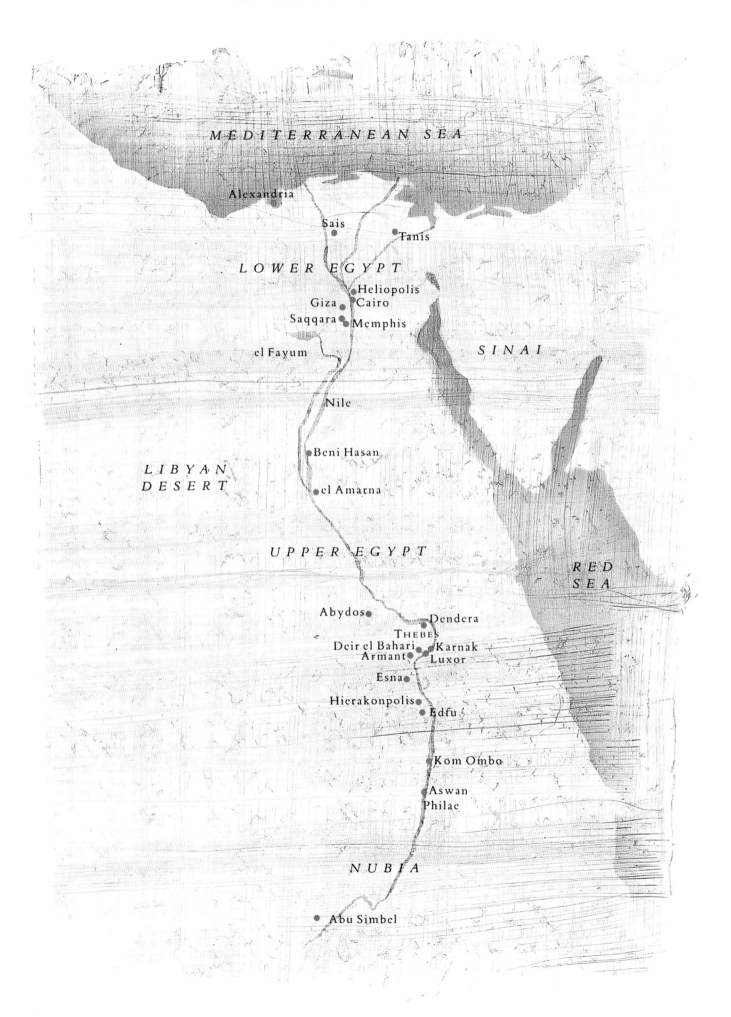

MEDITERRANEAN SEA

Alexandria

Sais

Tanis

LOWER EGYPT

Heliopolis
Cairo
Giza
Saqqara
Memphis

el Fayum

SINAI

Nile

Beni Hasan

el Amarna

LIBYAN
DESERT

UPPER EGYPT

RED
SEA

Abydos

Dendera
THEBES
Deir el Bahari
Karnak
Armant
Luxor

Esna

Hierakonpolis
Edfu

Kom Ombo

Aswan
Philae

NUBIA

Abu Simbel

engineer. These skills led him to become involved in the removal of a colossal bust of Ramses II which he successfully transported to the British Museum in 1818. This project was commissioned by Henry Salt, who was the British Consul in Egypt. Salt himself became a keen collector of Egyptian antiquities and his collection, with the help of Belzoni, was to form the nucleus of that of the British Museum. They were both involved in lengthy and frustrating financial negotiations with the trustees of the Museum who disputed the value of some of the sculpture. The main problem was that many people regarded Egyptian statues as greatly inferior to Classical, being merely curiosities rather than works of art. Belzoni went on to complete some successful excavations in Egypt, discovering an entrance to the Second Pyramid and the Tomb of Seti I, in the Valley of the Kings. He also travelled far south to the great temple of Abu Simbel in Nubia, which he was the first to enter since ancient times. He published a popular account of these exploits in four different languages and staged a spectacular exhibition at the Egyptian Hall in Piccadilly, in 1821.

Sir John Gardner Wilkinson is generally regarded as the founder of British Egyptology. He spent many years in Egypt copying paintings and inscriptions and mastering the ancient language. He was the first to attempt placing

the inhabitants were not particularly friendly to Europeans, while the climate and prevalence of serious diseases added to the difficulty.

The most colourful personality to be involved with Egyptology at this time was an Italian called Giovanni Belzoni. He had been a strongman performer in the London theatre and had travelled to Egypt to work as an

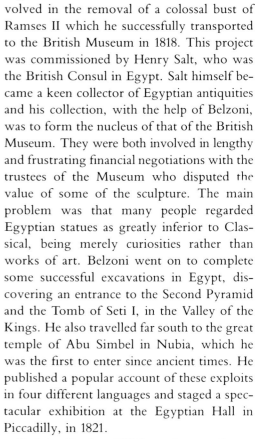

the royal dynasties and kings into proper date order and gave many important antiquities to the British Museum. He popularized Egyptology with his best-known book *The Manners and Customs of the Ancient Egyptians* (1837) which became the standard work on religion, daily life and culture for many years. Another key figure in Egyptology at this time was Robert Hay, who like Wilkinson was not funded by any organization. He financed a number of important expeditions resulting in detailed studies.

This essential, serious survey work eventually gained official interest and, in the 1840s, the King of Prussia financed a large-scale expedition to the Nile. This was led by the capable Karl Lepsius who secured some major antiquities for the future Berlin Museum and produced a lavish publication of 24 volumes, entitled *Denkmaeler*. This is the largest work on Egyptology ever published and is still a valuable reference work for scholars today.

Egyptologists had been largely concerned with dating and language, and excavating had been undertaken in an unscientific way. Many inscriptions and papyri were destroyed in an eager search for more attractive antiquities, while unscrupulous dealers had little regard as to how they gained access to tombs. A Frenchman, called Auguste Mariette, who was collecting antiquities for the Louvre Museum, realized the need to prevent indiscriminate looting of sites and set up an official antiquities service for the Egyptians. Mariette ensured that excavation permits were only issued to qualified scholars and went on to found the Cairo Museum. A new standard of orderly, scientific archaeology was set by

ABOVE: *W.M.F. Petrie (1853–1942), the most active archaeologist working in Egypt, who pioneered new scientific methods and produced some 1,000 publications.*

A drawing by Giovanni Belzoni (1778–1823) showing the transport of a colossal bust of Ramses II which became part of the British Museum collection. Belzoni's successful direction of the transport of such a heavy statue to England was a remarkable achievement.

RIGHT: *Portrait of Henry Salt (1780–1827), the British Consul in Egypt whose important collection of antiquities formed the basis of the British Museum's Egyptian collection. (British Museum.)*

LEFT: *Coloured drawing of painted reliefs from the tomb of Seti I by Henry Salt (1780–1827), the British Consul in Egypt. He was a keen collector, responsible for obtaining some of the British Museum's major sculptures and also a skilled amateur artist. (British Museum.)*

W.M.F. Petrie, who excavated all over Egypt, publishing a detailed record and analysis of the finds almost every year between 1881 and 1925.

In the 1870s a pit was discovered at Thebes containing the mummies of most of the New Kingdom Pharaohs. These had been removed from their original tombs in antiquity by the priests and reburied to prevent their violation by tomb robbers. Archaeologists turned their attention to exploring the Valley of the Kings at Thebes to locate the original tombs. Howard Carter, a former assistant of Petrie, began excavating there in 1912 under the sponsorship of Lord Carnarvon. Eventually in 1922, he discovered the tomb of Tutankhamun, the first Pharaoh's tomb to be found virtually intact. The incredible wealth of gold and the superb artistic craftsmanship displayed

A COMPARATIVE CHRONOLOGY OF ANCIENT EGYPT

DATE	IN EGYPT	PERIOD	ELSEWHERE IN THE WORLD
500 AD	Last known demotic inscription Last hieroglyphic inscription Queen Zenobia of Palmyra occupies Egypt Bucolic War Alexandrian riots Death of Cleopatra	GRÆCO ROMAN PERIOD	Classical Mayan culture of Middle America Rome sacked Constantinople founded Middle Moche culture in South America Main building begins at Teotihuacan Jewish Diaspora Vesuvius engulfs Pompeii Claudian invasion of Britain
0	Temple built at Edfu Rebel native rulers at Thebes Ptolemy Lagos rules as Pharaoh Alexander the Great in Egypt Last native Pharaohs	PTOLEMAIC PERIOD DYNASTY 21–30 LATE DYNASTIC PERIOD	Birth of Christ Buddhism reaches China Julius Caesar invades Britain Destruction of Carthage Hannibal crosses Alps Start of unified Chinese Empire Death of Emperor Ashoka Alexander the Great in India Construction of Parthenon Defeat of Persians at Marathon
500 BC	Persians annex Egypt Greek colonies in Egypt Assyrian invasions Kushite kings rule Egypt Sheshonq I sacks Jerusalem Greatest power of Theban high priests		Birth of Buddha Nebuchadnezzar destroys Jerusalem Medes destroy Babylon Rise of cities in India Beginnings of Great Wall of China Rome founded First Olympic Games held Death of Solomon David rules from Jerusalem Chavin culture of South America
1000 BC	Extensive tomb robbing at Thebes Ramesses III repulses Sea Peoples Merneptah checks Libyan invasions Clashes with Hittites in Syria Tutankhamun returns to Thebes Akhenaten founds Akhetaten Luxor temple begun Tuthmosis III conquers Syria Queen Hatshepsut rules as Pharaoh	DYNASTY 18–20 NEW KINGDOM	Fall of Troy Olmec culture of Middle America Main building phase at Stonehenge Shang dynasty in China Fall of Knossos and Minoan Empire
1500 BC	First tomb in Valley of Kings Amosis expels Hyksos Thebans oppose Hyksos Hyksos seize Memphis Avaris becomes Hyksos capital Trade with Asia, Africa and Mediterranean Islands Karnak temple begun Fortresses built in Nubia New capital at Itj-tawy Mentuhotpe II reunites Egypt	DYNASTY 13–17 SECOND INTERMEDIATE PERIOD DYNASTY 11–12 MIDDLE KINGDOM	Hammurabi codifies law

A COMPARATIVE CHRONOLOGY OF ANCIENT EGYPT			
DATE	IN EGYPT	PERIOD	ELSEWHERE IN THE WORLD
2000 BC	Civil war between Thebes and Heracleopolis Pepi II reigns 94 years Unas pyramid first to contain text Sun temples at Abu Gurab Expeditions to Punt (Somalia)	DYNASTY 7–10 FIRST INTERMEDIATE PERIOD DYNASTY 3–6 OLD KINGDOM	First pottery made in Middle America Earliest smelting of iron in Middle East Indo-Europeans enter Anatolia Sargon of Agade Indus Valley Cultures of India Tablet archives at Ebla
2500 BC	Khufu builds Great Pyramid First true pyramid at Dahshur Step pyramid at Saqqara Expeditions to Sinai and Nubia Trade with Asia and tropical Africa First stone architectural elements	DYNASTY 1–2 ARCHAIC PERIOD	Royal burials at Ur
3000 BC	Invention of hieroglyphic writing Egypt united, Memphis founded Glazed composition made for first time Hard stone vessels produced Painted buff pottery	PRE DYNASTIC PERIOD NAQADA II CULTURE	First pottery made in South America Sumerians introduce writing
3500 BC	Stone vessels first produced White paint incised pottery First models of human figure Metal working practised Blacked topped red pottery first produced	NAQADA I CULTURE BADARIAN CULTURE	
4000 BC	Cereals and flax grown	EGYPTIAN STONE AGE	

in all this treasure attracted massive media coverage, which really captured peoples' imagination about Ancient Egypt.

Besides tombs, archaeologists excavated settlement sites in order to find out more about the Egyptians' daily life. The most important discoveries in this field have been at the ancient city of El-Amarna and the workmen's village of Deir el-Medina. At El-Amarna, a German team led by Ludwig Borchardt discovered the famous bust of Nefertiti, while excavating a sculptor's workshop. Large-scale archaeological surveys have been of great importance to Egyptology, initiated by the work of Norman de Garis Davies (1865–1941). He became the greatest copyist of Egyptian tombs and published more than 25 volumes on tombs alone, while his wife Nina made beautiful coloured reproductions of the wall-paintings. The most important work of this type to follow Davies was done by the University of Chicago who have a base at Luxor called The Chicago House. This organization, founded by James Breasted, has published an exhaustive record of the important temples at Medinet Habu and Abydos. Many specialized

ABOVE: *Howard Carter (1874–1939) and his team of archaeologists on horseback in the Valley of the Kings just before their famous discovery of Tutankhamun's tomb in 1922.*

societies have also been founded who sponsor excavations in Egypt and publish regular journals. One of the most famous is the Egypt Exploration Society which has a distinguished history of fieldwork and offers its members a means of keeping in touch with the latest developments in Egyptological research.

Although the treasures of Tutankhamun were handed over to the Cairo Museum, the Egyptian Government has been somewhat restrictive in granting permits to excavate since their discovery. They are naturally anxious not to lose any more of their cultural heritage, and scholars and museums have found sponsorship difficult since they are not allowed to keep what they excavate. From the 1950s onwards Egyptian universities and the Egyptian antiquities organizations have themselves excavated many sites and published an increasing amount of research material. However, in the 1960s the Egyptians appealed to the world to help them save their important Nubian monuments from the flooding due to the construction of the Aswan High Dam. An International Consortium of contractors and archaeologists was set up to move the

ABOVE: *Coloured engraving from Champoillon's epic publication* Monuments de l'Égypt *(1835–47) showing Ramses II in his chariot.*

BELOW: *Coloured engraving showing a Theban tomb painting from Rosellini's publication (1832–44) which recorded Egyptian monuments in great detail.*

throughout world museums. Understanding the language has always been of major importance to Egyptologists and they can learn a great deal from reading the large quantity of texts that have survived written on stone monuments, papyrus, and pottery and limestone ostraca fragments. The most useful textbook for students of the language is the famous *Egyptian Grammar* by Sir Alan Gardiner. First published in 1927, it has enabled generations of Egyptologists to study the hieroglyphic script. Great advances have been made in reading the difficult Demotic script and many texts await translation and publication. These may give us some fresh information about the Ancient Egyptians.

Nowadays, Ancient Egypt can be studied at various levels at universities, colleges, schools and adult education institutes. It can be taken as a separate degree subject or combined with Ancient History, Archaeology, Art History, Classics or Language Studies. Many museums, societies and adult education institutes also offer lecture programmes with slides, films and videos. Egypt itself is becoming increasingly popular and affordable to tourists and certain companies provide special study holidays with cruises down the Nile which have guest Egyptologists and expert guides to accompany the tours.

Modern Egyptologists have far greater study resources than their predecessors. They have dictionaries, lists of kings, and detailed site surveys to help them with their research.

ABOVE: *The Pyramids of Giza (c 2,500 BC).*

LEFT: *The gold mask of Tutankhamun (c 1,350 BC).*

RIGHT: *Head of Cleopatra (c 50 BC). (British Museum.)*

huge Temple of Abu-Simbel and some other monuments to higher ground.

The rescue project has inspired detailed surveys of sites under threat from the flood waters and greater interest in Nubia. Scholars now treat Nubian studies as a separate branch of Egyptology, with current research concentrating on the earliest settlements and the Kingdom of Meroe which survived into the fourth century AD.

Work in Egypt itself is only a small part of Egyptology and much has been achieved by studying collections of antiquities distributed

BOTTOM RIGHT: *Howard Carter and Lord Carnarvon at work in the tomb of Tutankhamun in 1922.*

ABOVE: *A view of the Ramesseum, Thebes in the 19th century by Francis Frith (1822–98), one of the most notable British pioneer photographers who travelled to Egypt.*

BELOW: *A watercolour drawing by the famous archaeologist Howard Carter (1874–1939) who was also an accomplished artist from a family of painters.*

LEFT: *Although there are only a few obelisks still standing in Egypt, there are over 50 in the public squares of capitals in Europe and America. (David Roberts lithograph c 1846).*

BELOW: *Egyptologists at work with a computer. Modern technology has aided the study of Egyptology.*

ABOVE: *August Mariette (1821–81) formed the Egyptian Antiquities service and founded the Cairo Museum. He directed many important excavations and published many books on Egyptology.*

RIGHT: *The Tomb of Queen Nefertari – watercolor copy by Nina Davies (1881–1965). Records like these are invaluable since many tomb paintings have deteriorated greatly since their discovery.*

Study of museum collections has also greatly improved through better documentation of the artefacts on computers and detailed photographic archives. Fresh knowledge can often be gained by using the latest scientific techniques to help with dating and analysis of the material. There is greater contact between Egyptologists internationally through specialist conferences and the current popularity of loan exhibitions of Egyptian antiquities.

Ancient Egypt covered a long period of history and a vast geographical area. So much has already been achieved by Egyptologists, yet there are some periods of history and many Pharaohs that we know little or nothing about. Research on existing collections is continuing and there must be countless antiquities still to be excavated and studied.

CHAPTER TWO

T*h e*
PYRAMIDS

ABOVE: *The Pyramids of Giza.*

Many people are unaware that any other pyramids exist besides the three at Giza. There are in fact remains of about 80 pyramids in Egypt, while there are well over 100 later, less substantial ones in the Sudan. However, the superior construction, scale and accessibility to Cairo of the Giza pyramids have made them the most famous. They are the only one of the Seven Wonders of the Ancient World still surviving.

Despite many fanciful theories, these pyramids were simply tombs of the Pharaohs. They all contained sarcophagi and are situated on the West Bank of the Nile where the Egyptians traditionally buried their dead. Like all pyramids they were built in groups and were part of a vast cemetery complex. This included mortuary temples and tombs of other members of the royal family and court and numerous priests and officials. Although the Giza pyramids are unique, their perfect form developed from earlier royal tomb structures.

Until the third dynasty, the traditional form of royal tomb was a mastaba. These were mainly large rectangular, flat-topped buildings with sloping sides. Beneath them were the burial chambers and rooms cut deep into the bedrock. Usually built in mud-brick, they were like architectural forms of prehistoric burial mounds. The earliest surviving pyramid, the famous Step Pyramid, at Saqqara, was itself originally conceived as a mastaba. At some stage the plans were altered, and the pyramid grew into a series of six progressively diminishing terraces.

The Step Pyramid was built around 2,650 BC for King Djoser by his chief architect Imhotep. It is the oldest large stone building in the world and Imhotep's great achievement led him to be revered by later generations as a god of wisdom. The Step Pyramid is the major feature in a vast complex of funerary architecture. These buildings and courtyards acted as a kind of stage set for the dead king to perform his funerary rites. They are of great importance, because, being made of stone they have survived, where most earlier mud-brick structures have disintegrated. They were originally enclosed by a wall some 1,500 feet long by 900 feet wide (500 by 300 metres). In its day, the sight of this wall of shining white limestone with the pyramid rising out of it must have been a majestic spectacle. Standing on the edge of a plateau overlooking

the ancient capital of Memphis, it must have represented a great symbol of the eternal power of their God King to the Egyptians who built it. Its clean, sharp edges have since been blurred through the passage of time and its finely worked limestone casing has been plundered, yet it is still impressive rising to a height of 200 feet (60 metres). The body of King Djoser was never found and like most tombs, the pyramid had been looted in ancient times. However, two alabaster sarcophagi were discovered, one containing the body of a child, while some 30,000 stone vases were also found in the precinct.

The pyramid underwent several stages of development in the next century before the Giza pyramids. Several miles south of Saqqara,

ABOVE: The Step Pyramid of King Djoser at Saqqara is the earliest surviving pyramid, built around 2,650 BC.

BELOW: The Step Pyramid adjacent to a Mastaba tomb from which its structure developed.

King Sneferu built the so-called 'Bent' Pyramid, which is not stepped but straight-sided, except for a curious change of angle in the middle. He built another pyramid at Maidum which seems originally to have been stepped then modified to become straight-sided. The outer courses of masonry collapsed in later times, leaving the curious structure which survives today. This has become merely a mound of sand and rubble surmounted by a tall tower which is actually the cone of the pyramid. Sneferu's son and successor was probably Khufu and he selected the imposing site at Giza to build the most perfect, impressive pyramid of all, the Great Pyramid.

The Great Pyramid in its original state rose 481 feet (160 metres) and is estimated to have contained 2,300,000 blocks of stone. Its vast size has prompted people to calculate some fascinating statistics. The area it covers is large enough to hold the cathedrals of Florence, Milan and St Peters in Rome, as well as St Pauls and Westminster Abbey in London. Napoleon estimated that the blocks of stone from the three Giza Pyramids would have been sufficient to build a wall of 10 feet (three metres) high and one foot (30 cm) thick around the whole of France. This claim was also verified by an eminent contemporary French mathematician.

The orientation of the Great Pyramid is incredibly accurate. The four sides, each of over 700 feet (230 metres) long, are aligned almost exactly on true north, south, east and

ABOVE: *The Pyramids of Giza – The Great Pyramid of Khufu (far left) and the Pyramids of Khafra (centre) and Mankaura (right) – the three much smaller pyramids in front belonged to queens.*

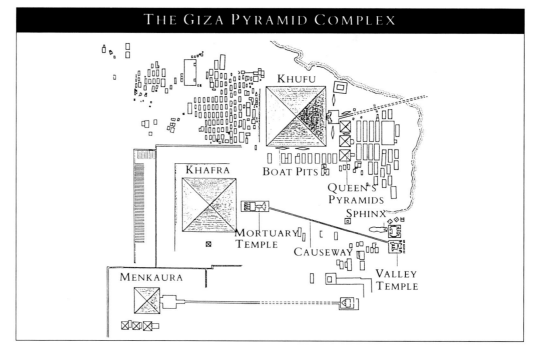

THE GIZA PYRAMID COMPLEX

KHUFU

KHAFRA

BOAT PITS

QUEEN'S PYRAMIDS

SPHINX

MORTUARY TEMPLE

CAUSEWAY

MENKAURA

VALLEY TEMPLE

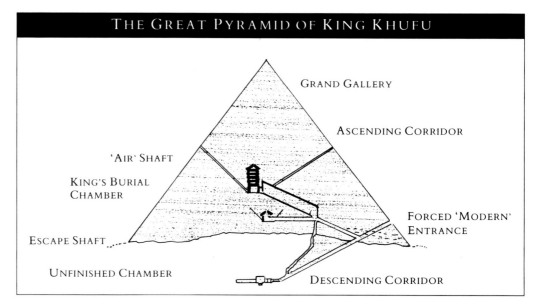

THE GREAT PYRAMID OF KING KHUFU

GRAND GALLERY

ASCENDING CORRIDOR

'AIR' SHAFT

KING'S BURIAL CHAMBER

FORCED 'MODERN' ENTRANCE

ESCAPE SHAFT

UNFINISHED CHAMBER

DESCENDING CORRIDOR

PYRAMID CONSTRUCTION

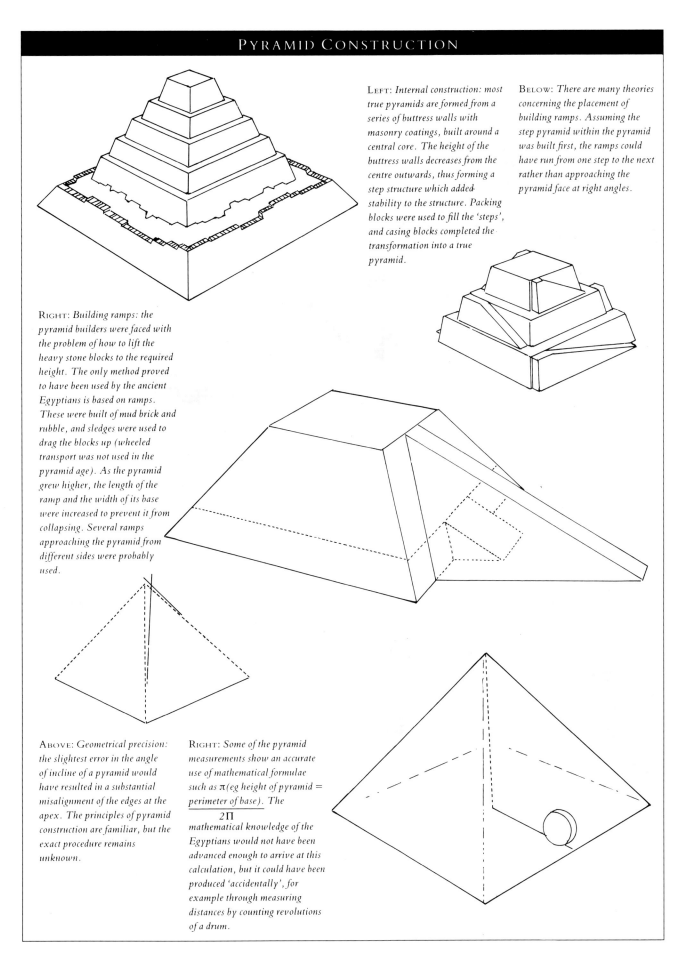

LEFT: *Internal construction: most true pyramids are formed from a series of buttress walls with masonry coatings, built around a central core. The height of the buttress walls decreases from the centre outwards, thus forming a step structure which added stability to the structure. Packing blocks were used to fill the 'steps', and casing blocks completed the transformation into a true pyramid.*

BELOW: *There are many theories concerning the placement of building ramps. Assuming the step pyramid within the pyramid was built first, the ramps could have run from one step to the next rather than approaching the pyramid face at right angles.*

RIGHT: *Building ramps: the pyramid builders were faced with the problem of how to lift the heavy stone blocks to the required height. The only method proved to have been used by the ancient Egyptians is based on ramps. These were built of mud brick and rubble, and sledges were used to drag the blocks up (wheeled transport was not used in the pyramid age). As the pyramid grew higher, the length of the ramp and the width of its base were increased to prevent it from collapsing. Several ramps approaching the pyramid from different sides were probably used.*

ABOVE: *Geometrical precision: the slightest error in the angle of incline of a pyramid would have resulted in a substantial misalignment of the edges at the apex. The principles of pyramid construction are familiar, but the exact procedure remains unknown.*

RIGHT: *Some of the pyramid measurements show an accurate use of mathematical formulae such as π (eg height of pyramid =*

$$\frac{\text{perimeter of base}}{2\Pi}$$

mathematical knowledge of the Egyptians would not have been advanced enough to arrive at this calculation, but it could have been produced 'accidentally', for example through measuring distances by counting revolutions of a drum.

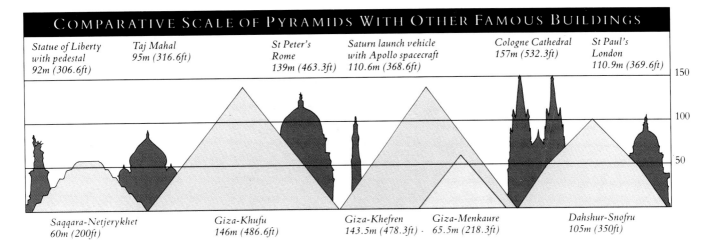

COMPARATIVE SCALE OF PYRAMIDS WITH OTHER FAMOUS BUILDINGS					
Statue of Liberty with pedestal 92m (306.6ft)	Taj Mahal 95m (316.6ft)	St Peter's Rome 139m (463.3ft)	Saturn launch vehicle with Apollo spacecraft 110.6m (368.6ft)	Cologne Cathedral 157m (532.3ft)	St Paul's London 110.9m (369.6ft)

Saqqara-Netjerykhet 60m (200ft) Giza-Khufu 146m (486.6ft) Giza-Khefren 143.5m (478.3ft) Giza-Menkaure 65.5m (218.3ft) Dahshur-Snofru 105m (350ft)

west. These alignments are so accurate that compass errors can be checked against them. This is an amazing achievement considering the magnetic compass was unknown to the Ancient Egyptians. They probably managed to obtain such accuracy by observing a northern star, rising and setting. The cardinal points, north and south, could have been established by taking measurements with a plumb line.

The millions of blocks of stone which make up the pyramid are of three main types from three sources. The great bulk of stone which forms the core is a poor quality limestone which occurs naturally in the near vicinity. Much finer white limestone casing blocks which originally covered its entire surface were mined at Tura further up the Nile. The heaviest blocks, some weighing over 50 tons, used for lining the internal chambers and passages, are made of granite quarried at Aswan some 500 miles (800 km) away. Nearly all the

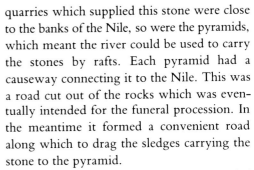

LEFT: *King Khafra, builder of the second pyramid at Giza, reflects in his proud face the supreme power of the Pharaoh in the Old Kingdom. The hawk spreading his wings protectively around the Pharaoh's head represents Horus, the god associated with kingship. (c 2540 BC.) (Cairo Museum.)*

BOTTOM: *The pyramid at Maidum represents the transitional stage of development from the step pyramid to the true pyramid. It was originally conceived as a step pyramid and subsequently modified to a true pyramid by additional casing, but the enormous pressures thus created led to its partial collapse.*

quarries which supplied this stone were close to the banks of the Nile, so were the pyramids, which meant the river could be used to carry the stones by rafts. Each pyramid had a causeway connecting it to the Nile. This was a road cut out of the rocks which was eventually intended for the funeral procession. In the meantime it formed a convenient road along which to drag the sledges carrying the stone to the pyramid.

The supply of so much stone demanded intensive quarrying. The Ancient Egyptians possessed little more than primitive copper chisels so they must have developed a specialized technique for extracting the stone. It was easier to cut the softer limestone than the hard granite. The poorer quality limestone was extracted quite easily by open-cast quarrying since it lay on the surface. However, tunnelling was required to obtain the finer Tura limestone and the granite. This was probably assisted by the application of heat and water. Wooden wedges were driven into cracks in the stone then soaked in water, causing them to expand and separate the stone. The blocks were then squared up using chisels and mallets. Copper saws were also used, perhaps with jewel chippings to assist the cutting. In order to work the granite they had to pound it with balls of an even harder stone called dolerite. Although the majority of limestone blocks which formed the core were only roughly finished, the facing stones had to be cut with great precision. Most of these have since been looted by the stonemasons of Cairo, but those which remain at the base, where sand covered them, fit so closely that the joints are almost invisible. They would have been smoothed off after they were put in place when the building of the pyramid was completed.

ABOVE: *19th-century photograph of the Sphinx, which represents King Khafra with a lion's powerful body. In the background is his pyramid tomb.*

RIGHT: *Bronze statuette of Imhotep, the architect of the earliest step pyramid at Saqqara. In later times Imhotep was worshipped as a god of wisdom. (c 600 BC.) (British Museum.)*

Enormous ancient waste dumps of limestone chippings from working the blocks have been discovered nearby. It has been estimated that the stone from these dumps is of an equivalent volume to over half that of the pyramids.

There is no contemporary written evidence surviving that describes how the pyramids were built. The Greek historian Herodotus, who visited Egypt in the fifth century BC, claimed that gangs of 100,000 workmen, rotating in shifts of three months each, toiled for 20 years building the Great Pyramid. Egyptologists now believe that it was built in less time by fewer men. Many people are under the false impression that the pyramids were built by slaves for a tyrannical Pharaoh. It is unlikely that the Egyptians had any slaves at this time as their society was largely com-

ABOVE: *19th-century photograph showing tourists being helped to climb the stones of the Great Pyramid. The pyramid was robbed of its fine limestone outer casing over the years and the interlocking blocks form a series of climbable, irregular steps.*

posed of peasant farmers. For three months of the year, during the inundation season, the men were unable to work in the fields and would therefore be idle anyway. The concerted effort of these peasant farmers to build their Pharaoh's tomb was justified by their belief that he was a god. The Pharaoh was thought to be the Son of the Sun, who had taken human form to lead the people whom he would continue to assist in the Next World.

Peasant farmers carried out the purely physical labour but there must have been many skilled workers engaged in this vast building project. The large demand for stone would require specialist quarrymen. They worked in gangs and many stones have their names still painted on them such as 'Boat Gang', 'South Gang' and 'Enduring Gang'. The stone

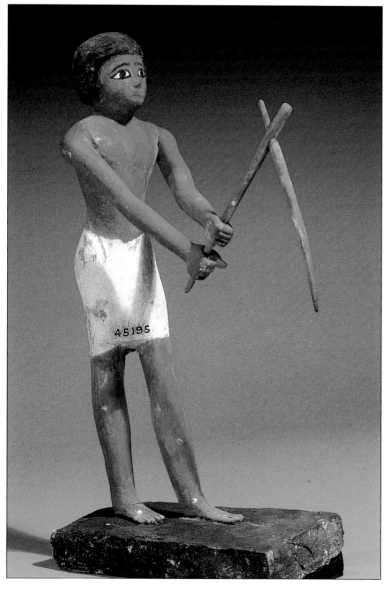

would still have to be worked into blocks and finished by stonemasons. Men with building skills would be needed to lay the blocks level and close together. The majority of the workforce was involved in moving the stone only when they couldn't work the fields, but these more specialist workers would be employed permanently on the pyramid or in the quarries. Near the Great Pyramid, barracks or lodgings for 4,000 men have been excavated. From the tools discovered there it is likely that they were occupied by builders and stonemasons working on the pyramids.

Our ideas as to how the Great Pyramid was constructed can only be based on speculation. A great deal of survey and planning work would have been necessary before any building took place. Surviving sketches of other buildings suggest that they would have made plans, and limestone models of different pyramids exist which may represent architectural planning aids. The site would need to be completely level before work commenced. They probably gauged this with accuracy by digging a trench of water around the square perimeter. Some knowledge of mathematics, geometry and astronomy would also be required for calculating the angles of the pyramid. It is certain that the various courses of stone were laid from the centre outwards since there are places where the central core blocks have been exposed beneath the casing blocks. It is also evident that they smoothed these final casing blocks from the top downwards. We do not know how the blocks were raised

from ground level to their final position. It is likely that massive supply and construction ramps were built round the building area. The heavy blocks would have been dragged up these ramps on sleds to the working platform. The remains of ramps have been discovered at the Maidum Pyramid. They may also have used a kind of scaffolding for dressing it with limestone.

Throughout history, the huge mass of stone of the Great Pyramid has inspired people to believe that many secrets lie hidden within it. The early Christians believed the pyramids to be the granaries of Joseph, while generations of Arabs were convinced that they contained fantastic treasure. Despite various structural security measures, the burial treasure they did contain was looted when tomb robbers broke in, probably before 2000 BC. The interior of

the Great Pyramid consists of an approach passage and the burial chamber itself. The slanted roof and cross-beams of granite in the burial chamber are to support the colossal weight above it. The passage leading to it is wider at the top to enable the narrower entrance to be sealed with giant plug blocks of granite. The design of the interior only appears complicated because the location of the burial chamber was changed twice during its construction. The two so-called 'ventilation shafts' may have been a symbolic means of exit for the dead king's spirit. Later pyramid texts describe the king as mounting heaven on the rays of the sun. The pyramid itself could have represented the rays of the sun shining down on earth. Perhaps it was also conceived, like the Babylonian Ziggurat, as a sort of stairway to heaven.

C H A P T E R   T H R E E

T*he*
PHARAOHS

ABOVE: *A fine early ivory
standing figure of a king
discovered at Abydos,
probably dating from the
First Dynasty c 3000 BC.
The Pharaoh wears the
white crown of Upper
Egypt and a long robe
which was worn at his
jubilee. (British Museum.)*

The word Pharaoh comes from the Egyptian 'Per-aa', meaning Great House and originally referred to the palace rather than the king himself. It was used by the biblical writers and has become widely adopted since as a special word for the King of Egypt. The Pharaoh had several official titles which related to his unique status as being both god and king. He was referred to as the son of the god Ra and the name of Ra is usually mentioned within his two royal seals or cartouches, along with his personal name. He was also believed to be the incarnation of the god Horus, the son of Osiris, who in Ancient Egyptian mythology was the first King of the World.

The Pharaoh is also constantly referred to as being the Lord of the Two Lands. In early times the people of Egypt were gathered in the north and south and the unification of these two geographical regions under one Pharaoh became a primary event in Ancient Egyptian history. Although a new capital was established at Memphis, there continued to be a northern and southern centre of government administration and throughout Ancient Egyptian history there is evidence of a deep-seated awareness that the one nation had been formed out of the Two Lands. The Ancient Egyptians achieved a national unity through the Pharaoh, which brought them all the benefits of a centralized nation and enabled efficient irrigation, land reclamation and pyramid building. The Great Pyramid could only have been built by a king who exercised complete control over the economic resources of the country. The large quantities of stone, the unlimited manpower and the skill of the finest craftsmen were all at the Pharaoh's disposal. King Khufu must have been the most powerful Pharaoh at that time and his pyramid is the greatest. The decreasing size of the other two probably indicate the diminishing power of successive kings. After the collapse of royal power at the end of the Old Kingdom, the successive Pharaohs in the Middle Kingdom had to contend with the increased strength and arrogance of the provincial governors. The country was divided into a number of administrative districts called 'nomes' under these governors who had transformed their offices into hereditary principalities. Perhaps to limit their power, the Middle Kingdom kings developed a centralized hierarchy, and the royal residence was moved from Thebes

HIEROGLYPHIC WRITINGS OF SELECTED ROYAL NAMES

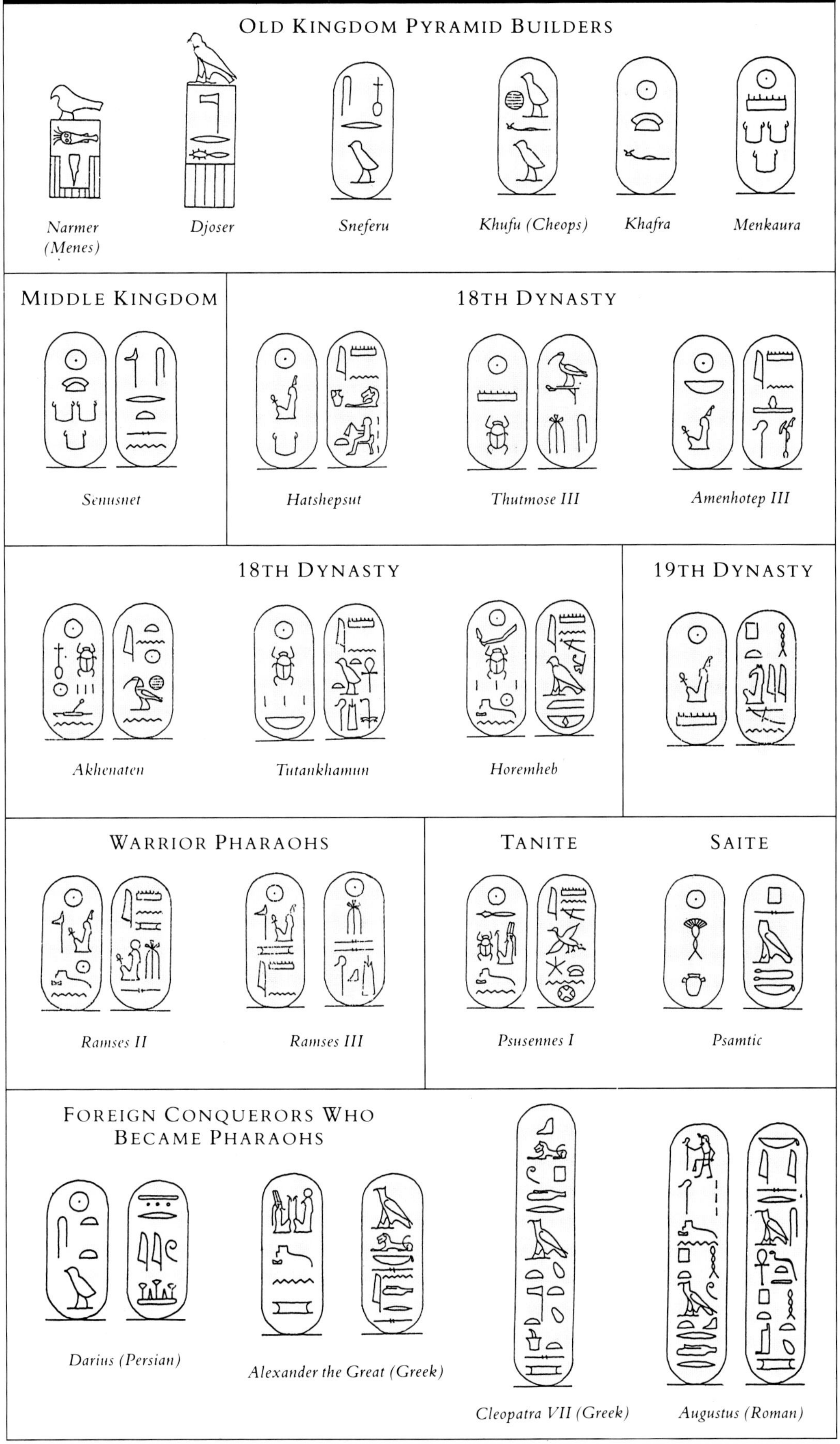

OLD KINGDOM PYRAMID BUILDERS

Narmer
(Menes)

Djoser

Sneferu

Khufu (Cheops)

Khafra

Menkaura

MIDDLE KINGDOM

Senusret

18TH DYNASTY

Hatshepsut

Thutmose III

Amenhotep III

18TH DYNASTY

Akhenaten

Tutankhamun

Horemheb

19TH DYNASTY

WARRIOR PHARAOHS

Ramses II

Ramses III

TANITE

SAITE

Psusennes I

Psamtic

FOREIGN CONQUERORS WHO BECAME PHARAOHS

Darius (Persian)

Alexander the Great (Greek)

Cleopatra VII (Greek)

Augustus (Roman)

to Lisht, which was a more convenient centre for ruling the whole country. These reforms enabled King Senusret III to raise a sizeable army for his Nubian campaigns, when the frontier was moved further south and was protected by a network of fortresses. In another campaign he increased the hold Egypt already had over Palestine and Syria. During the short reigns of some 70 weaker kings of the thirteenth dynasty (c1786–1633 BC), bureaucracy increased and the lack of a strong government enabled a group of Asiatics called the Hyksos to invade and control Egypt for some hundred years. The Hyksos immigrants introduced some important technical innovations – bronze-working, the horse and chariot, and other weapons of war such as more powerful bows.

The first Pharaohs of the New Kingdom drove out the Hyksos rulers and unified the state with a much improved economy. They went on to extend Egyptian territories into Western Asia as far as the Euphrates. The Egyptian 'Empire', which included the city states of Syria and Palestine, paid tribute but remained self-governing while Nubia was

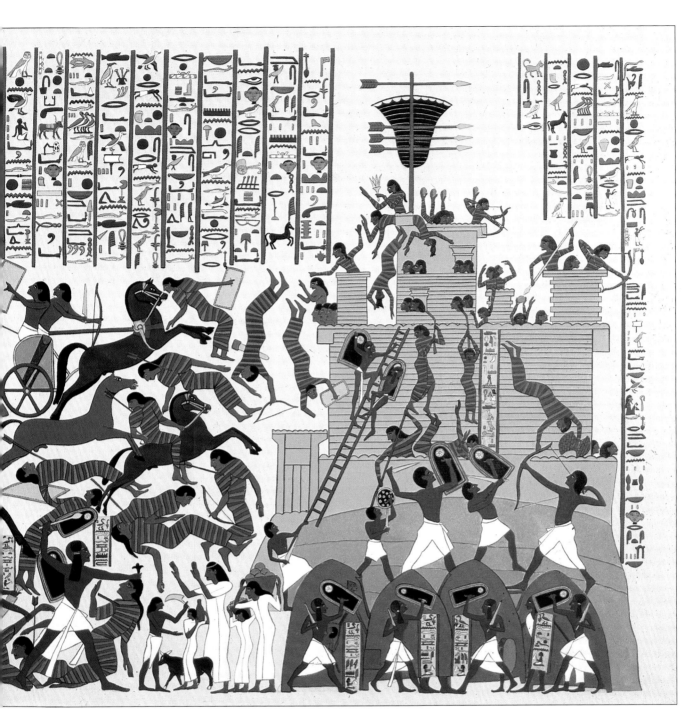

ABOVE: *Ramses II in his chariot attacks the Hittite fortress of Dapur, in Syria – reconstruction of a painted relief from the Ramesseum, Thebes, c 1,270 BC.*

administered directly by the Egyptians through an appointed Viceroy. Trade and Nubian gold produced much of the country's wealth and power in international relations and the surviving royal burial treasures display unprecedented wealth and aesthetic beauty.

The Pharaohs of the New Kingdom, and in particular those of the eighteenth dynasty, have aroused the greatest popular interest. One of the first notable Pharaohs during this period was in fact a woman, called Hatshepsut. She ruled as the dominant partner and personality in a co-regency with her nephew and

stepson, the young Thutmose III. She is frequently depicted on statues and reliefs with the male attributes of royalty including the false beard. During her reign, Senenmut the chief steward assumed a position of great power as her favourite and supervised the building of her magnificent temple at Deir el Bahari in Thebes.

Thutmost III continued the policy of foreign conquest with campaigns in Palestine, Syria and Nubia. Many impressive buildings and important private tombs were created during his reign which are a sign of the economic

ABOVE: *Queen
Hatshepsut's Temple, a
complex of colonnaded
shrines, rises in terraces to
the cliffs at Deir el Bahri.*

BELOW: *Standing statue of
a Pharaoh from the Middle
Kingdom – his thoughtful
and concerned expression is
characteristic of the style of
portrayal during this
period. (British Museum.)*

benefits of his imperialistic policy. Late in his
reign he turned against the memory of Hatshepsut and ordered many of her statues and
reliefs to be defaced or usurped by his own
name and image. His actions were perhaps
due to the Egyptian concept of kingship as
being exclusively male, rather than to personal hatred of his aunt.

Under Amenhotep III, Egypt continued to
be acknowledged as a superior power by her
Asiatic neighbours. In Syria, the kingdom of
Mitanni sent princesses as a gift of tribute to
the Pharaoh and peace brought great prosperity to Egypt. There was an unprecedented
output of architecture and sculpture on a grand
scale during his reign, much of it of superb
quality. He was succeeded by Amenhotep IV
who is more commonly known by the name
Akhenaten from his association with the sun
cult of Aten. Akhenaten came to be regarded
as the 'heretic Pharaoh' since he broke with a
long-established religious tradition of worshipping many gods, choosing instead to
adopt a single faith. He believed that the Aten
was the universal creator of all life and its

visible symbol was the rays of the sun. He became totally preoccupied with spreading his new faith and he neglected affairs of the state and military involvement. In order to disassociate himself from the powerful existing priesthood at Thebes, he built a completely new city some 200 miles (300 km) down the river at El Amarna. Here he built a palace to house his court and Amarna became the new capital and religious centre for the worship of the Aten.

Akhenaten appears to have been very interested in the arts and besides composing various hymns to the god Aten, he encouraged the development of an entirely new, more naturalistic art style. Unfortunately, very little has survived, since after his death he was pro-

claimed a heretic and his city was systematically destroyed and his monuments defaced. However, several pieces of royal portrait sculpture were discovered, among them the bust of Nefertiti which has come to be regarded as one of the most famous Ancient Egyptian works of art. Various diplomatic correspondence has also been discovered at Amarna which reveals the disorder within the Egyptian Empire. There are pleas for assistance from royal kingdoms under attack from the Hittites which the Pharaoh appears to have ignored.

ABOVE: *The so-called Colossi of Memnon: gigantic seated statues of the Pharaoh Amenhotep III, originally part of his mortuary temple at Thebes, c 1,400 BC. (British Museum.)*

LEFT: *Quartzite head from a statue of King Amenhotep III, c 1,400 BC. (British Museum.)*

After Akhenaten's death, the heir to the throne was Tutankhaten whose exact relationship to him has not been fully established. When Nefertiti died shortly after Akhenaten, the priests of Amun seized the opportunity to persuade the boy king to renounce his faith and reinstate the worship of the original gods at Thebes. To acknowledge this, the ending of his name was changed and he then became known as Tutankhamun. The old ways were gradually restored, and the city of Amarna was abandoned for Thebes. The usual preparations were made for the Pharaoh's tomb in the Valley of the Kings at Thebes but he died young, before its completion. It was therefore necessary to bury him in a make-shift tomb whose modesty and less obvious location caused it to be overlooked by the tomb

successfully resisted the Hittites with whom he signed a peace treaty. He instigated a vast programme of building and his Temple at Abydos contains numerous superb bas-reliefs which are regarded by many as the finest examples of Egyptian Art. This style of relief sculpture was also used to decorate this tomb which is the largest and most beautiful in the Valley of the Kings. Towards the end of his reign Seti I shared his throne with his son Ramses II who became the greatest Pharaoh of all.

Ramses began his reign with a military campaign in Syria where he fought the Hittites at the notorious battle of Qadesh. There are numerous depictions of the battle on temple reliefs which show it to be a great Egyptian victory, but it is generally believed to have been an indecisive battle. Shortly after it, a truce was made, which was confirmed by marriages between Ramses and Hittite princesses, and this continued for over 50 years. Ramses may have used art as a means of propaganda and his victories over foreigners are depicted on numerous temple reliefs while he had more colossal statues than any other Pharaoh. He also usurped many existing statues by inscribing his own cartouche on them. This same cartouche is carved on every significant group of ruins in Egypt and probably half the surviving temples have additions by him. Many of these great building projects date from his early years and it appears that there was considerable economic decline towards the end of his long 66-year reign. He was nearly 100 years old when he died and was the father of about 90 children from numerous wives. Of the nine succeeding kings who have the same name, Ramses III is probably the most notable. He inherited a stable internal situation and built an impressive and beautifully decorated temple complex at Medinet Habu. He managed to defeat an attempted Libyan invasion and renewed attacks by the so-called Sea Peoples of the Mediterranean.

Throughout the New Kingdom the authority of the Pharaoh was affected by two new forces in Egypt's internal politics, the priesthood and the army. The king as the traditional protector of Egypt was assisted in police and military matters by an army. The armies of the New Kingdom were far greater and more organized than in previous times with their chariots, infantry and marines. The army was

robbers. Although it was broken into hurriedly and with little loss early on, it remained intact for more than 3,000 years. The immense publicity the discovery of his tomb received in 1922, and the sheer wealth and beauty of the artefacts has made this historically insignificant boy king the most famous Pharaoh of all.

Tutankhamun left no heir to succeed him and an important and powerful official called Ay briefly became Pharaoh. He was followed by a successful general called Horemheb and under him all trace of the Akhenaten heresy was erased from Egyptian history. The city of Amarna was destroyed and the royal cartouches of Akhenaten and Tutankhamun were erased from the Temple records.

The first notable Pharaoh of the nineteenth dynasty (*c*1320–1200 BC) was Seti who consolidated Egyptian power in Palestine and

ABOVE: Upper part of a large statue of Akhenaten (Cairo Museum). This is a stylized portrait of the most mysterious and individual of all the Ancient Egyptian Pharaohs.

RIGHT: Painted plaster bust of Queen Nefertiti. Carved in the naturalistic style used during the reign of her husband King Akhenaten, this is one of the most beautiful and famous images in Egyptian Art. c 1,365 BC. (W. Berlin Museum.)

considered qualified to take over kingship at various times during the eighteenth dynasty when the Pharaoh had no direct heirs. Ay, Horemheb, Ramses I and Seti I had all had military training and when the country was drifting into anarchy in later periods, army officers stepped in to restore order.

By the 21st dynasty (c1085–945 BC) the country had become divided between two ruling houses. A group of kings established a new capital at Tanis in the Delta while much of Upper Egypt was controlled by generals who made themselves the High Priests of Thebes. A significant Pharaoh during this period was Psusennes I. The beautiful treasures from his tomb, which were discovered by Pierre Montet at Tanis in 1941, have been compared in their quality and richness to those of Tutankhamun. Political weaknesses soon led to foreign domination, first by the Libyan Kings of the 22nd dynasty, followed by the Ethiopians of Nubia in the 25th dynasty. The Pharaohs of the next dynasty established a new capital at Sais and restored order in Egypt. During this period of economic stability and greater prosperity (c664–525 BC) there was a rebirth of art, architecture and literature influenced by the earlier periods of Egyptian history. Some of the art of this period reached a highly stylized perfection and there was a tremendous output of fine quality small-scale sculpture.

The rule of the Saite Pharaohs was brought to a close by the Persian invasion and domination during the 27th dynasty. In 332 BC Alexander the Great conquered Egypt and his principal general, Ptolemy, set up a dynasty of Pharaohs based at Alexandria. This new city on the Mediterranean coast became a major trading centre and its famous lighthouse and library made it a Wonder of the Ancient World. The Greek domination of Egypt continued until Queen Cleopatra was defeated at the Battle of Actium in 31 BC and Egypt became a province of the Roman Empire. Through literary tradition, Cleopatra has captured popular imagination as a beautiful and scheming queen. She was the seventh Egyptian queen to bear the name of Cleopatra, and although her ancestry was Greek, she spoke the Egyptian language and shared some of their religious beliefs. Her affairs both with Julius Caesar and Mark Anthony and her final suicide were associated with her struggle to retain control of Egypt.

organized into four divisions of about 5,000 men each which gradually became composed of more mercenaries such as Nubians, Asiatics, Sea Peoples and Libyans. Prisoners of war could win freedom by taking up service in the Pharaoh's army and at the Battle of Qadesh, Ramses II's army included contingents of Mediterranean soldiers who had been captured in previous wars.

Although military strategy was always credited to the Pharaoh he would have consulted a War Council of officers and high state officials before embarking on a campaign. This kind of general staff would have great experience in controlling large numbers of men, which was probably why they were

ABOVE: *Queen wearing a characteristic royal 'vulture' head-dress – from a drawing by Howard Carter.*

LEFT: *Ramses wearing the most elaborate royal crown.*

RIGHT: *The Pharaoh Amenhotep III seated on a throne and wearing the blue crown.*

ROYAL CROWNS AND REGALIA

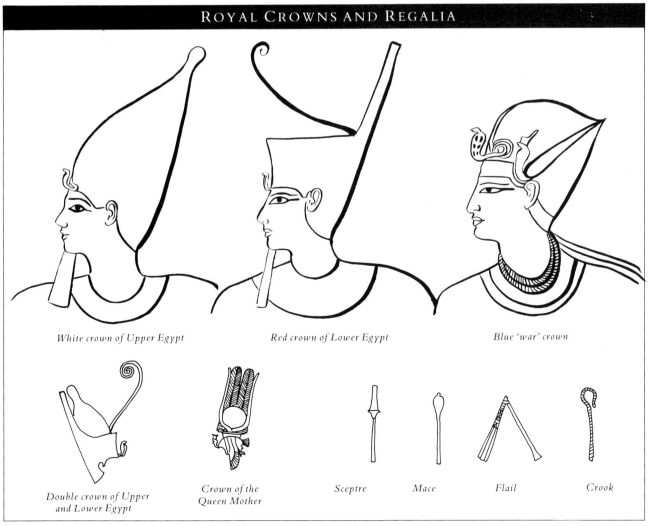

White crown of Upper Egypt

Red crown of Lower Egypt

Blue 'war' crown

Double crown of Upper and Lower Egypt

Crown of the Queen Mother

Sceptre

Mace

Flail

Crook

ABOVE: *Kneeling bronze figure of a Pharaoh offering two ointment jars. c 1,420 BC.*

LEFT: *King Tutankhamun and his queen from the back of his gilded throne. c 1,360 BC. (Cairo Museum.)*

ABOVE RIGHT: *Gilded wooden figure of a king, probably Amenhotep III, wearing a plaited wig. c 1,400 BC. (British Museum.)*

BELOW RIGHT: *Fragmentary statue of King Akhenaten. Many statues of the 'heretic' Pharaoh were systemically broken or destroyed after he died. (British Museum.)*

ABOVE: *Scene from Tutankhamun's painted box showing the king in his chariot hunting lions. (Cairo Museum.)*

LEFT: *Upper part of a colossal statue of Ramses II.*

Cleopatra ranks with Hatshepsut and Nefertiti as one of the best-known queens of Egypt. Some of the principal queens had a powerful position in Egyptian society, second only to the Pharaoh. The king was allowed to marry several wives, but the most important was called the 'Great Wife' and her children were usually the only heirs to the throne. Queen Hatshepsut was the daughter of King Thutmose I and his 'Great Wife'. The 'Mother of the King' continued her title as wife and queen when her son became Pharaoh but she became subordinate to the new king's principal consort, the 'Great Wife'. The eldest son of the Pharaoh by this principal queen often became his heir. Intermarriage among the Egyptian royal families was not as widespread as has been claimed and was really a political union to contain power within the family and reinforce succession.

Royal pedigree was not an essential qualification for kingship in Ancient Egypt and the

divine nature of the Pharaoh's office rendered any mortal connection secondary. The king's accession to the throne was justified by his claim to be son of the sun god, Ra, rather than son of a preceding king. In taking up the very office of Pharaoh he had in effect an unquestionable right to the throne of Egypt. Ay and Horemheb had no royal pedigree, yet they each succeeded Tutankhamun and could justify their kingship through this principle. Certain foreign conquerors, notably the Macedonian Greeks, realized the benefits of depicting themselves as traditional native Pharaohs in statues and on monuments throughout Egypt. They also had their names translated and placed in the customary royal cartouche and thereby claimed their divine ancestry alongside preceding kings. They were able to gain the maximum revenue from the country that they or their predecessors had conquered by assuming this supreme position of both god and king.

RIGHT: *Head, probably of Queen Hatshepsut, carved from fine green schist, wearing a tall white crown. (British Museum.)*

43

CHAPTER FOUR

The
GODS

ABOVE: *Silver figure of the god Ra with a falcon head and sun disc. (British Museum.)*

The gods of Ancient Egypt may appear to be strange and even frightening but to the Egyptians themselves they were an essential and comforting part of their daily life. Their apparent worship of animals should not be taken too literally since animals could be used as convenient and familiar symbols to represent the attributes of various gods. Animal heads were placed on human bodies as a means of showing gods performing various rituals and relating them to human actions. The worship of gods in the form of animals dates back to the earliest times in Egypt, and may have been motivated by man's fear of animals and their usefulness to him. These early disorganized societies viewed the natural order of the animal kingdom with awe as being symbolic of divine power. Particular animal qualities like the strength of the lion, the ferocity of the crocodile or the tender care of the cow for her young were revered and came to be associated with human ideals.

As time went on many gods came to be depicted in human form but still retained their identification with particular animals. By the late period almost every animal known to them was associated with one or more gods. Sacred creatures ranging in size from beetles to bulls were mummified and ceremonially buried. Vast animal cemeteries were created at various centres of cult worship and here people could show their devotion to a god by paying for the burial of its sacred animal. The opportunity for ordinary people to make offerings to the major gods only existed in later Egyptian history. Access to the temple interior was denied to everyone except the priesthood and only after the Middle Kingdom (c2000 BC) were privileged people allowed to place votive statues in the outer courtyards. In general, the images of the gods were inaccessible to the Egyptian people and any communication with them was exclusive to the Pharaoh or priests acting for him. The king was believed to be a supreme being who maintained the unity and prosperity of Egypt. The destiny of the Egyptian people was linked to that of their Pharaoh and his welfare was also theirs. Worshipping their king was a means to encourage him to intercede with other gods on their behalf.

The massive Egyptian temples were not intended for community worship like European cathedrals, and their main function was as the home of the gods. The temple with its

gateway, courts and halls was built around one small room, the sanctuary, housing the statue used by the god as its resting place. These statues did leave the temples for special religious festivals when they could be approached by ordinary people but their images were still hidden in a shrine carried on a sacred boat. Daily rituals in the temple included the washing and clothing of this divine statue and making offerings before it of incense and food. The significance of this ritual was symbolically to maintain the divine order of daily life and it does not represent blatant idol worship. In the carved reliefs in

ABOVE: *The Temple was the home of the gods and needed to be of superhuman proportions. The columns of the Great Temple of Karnak are 79 feet (31.6 metres) high and 12 feet (4.8 metres) in diameter in places.*

the temple, the king himself is always shown performing these rituals, but in practice they would usually have been taken over by priests. Such reliefs were usually carved with great skill and often occur even at the top of walls and columns where they could not be seen. They were not intended to beautify the building or inspire the worshippers but had an entirely magical function. In addition, the columns, ceilings and floors were all thought to have magical powers that could be invoked by rituals.

The temple was not only seen as a symbolic representation of the world but was also built

as a model of its creation. The wavy tiers of mud brick walls surrounding the sacred precinct probably represented the primeval waters while inside the enclosure the rows of papyrus and lotus-shaped columns symbolized the earliest marsh vegetation. In Egyptian mythology, this marsh represented the first solid matter, or mound, on which the god Ra appeared and created a pair of deities, Shu and Tefnut, by masturbation or spitting. They in turn produced the sky goddess Nut, and the earth god Geb whose children were the more familiar gods Osiris, Isis, Nephthys and Set. This group of nine gods 'ennead' were worshipped at Heliopolis, and other centres had similar groups of gods. Heliopolis was also the most important centre of the cult of the sun god Ra, who was described in many texts as the creator of everything.

The sun played a central part in religious beliefs throughout Egyptian history. The sun god Ra became important as early as the second dynasty (c2,700 BC) and almost certainly had some connection with the building of the pyramids. By the fifth dynasty (c2,400 BC) Ra had become the supreme state god who was closely associated with the Pharaoh. The king took the title Son of Ra and it was

ABOVE: *Ramses II kneels before the supreme god Amen Ra in the presence of his father Seti I and the moon god Khonsu and the mother goddess Mut.*

BELOW: *Ramses II statues in the forecourt of Luxor Temple.*

RIGHT: *The god Osiris – King of the Dead, protected by falcons – from a painted coffin c 1,050 BC. (British Museum.)*

believed that after death he also joined his father Ra in heaven. Another belief was that the sun god was born every morning, aged and died, then travelled through the underworld during the night, and this was seen as the model for all regeneration. Ra was united with a minor Theban god called Amun to produce Amen-Ra who became the supreme state god in the New Kingdom. From early times Ra was also associated with the hawk god Horus and the composite god Ra-Harakhty represented Horus of the horizon.

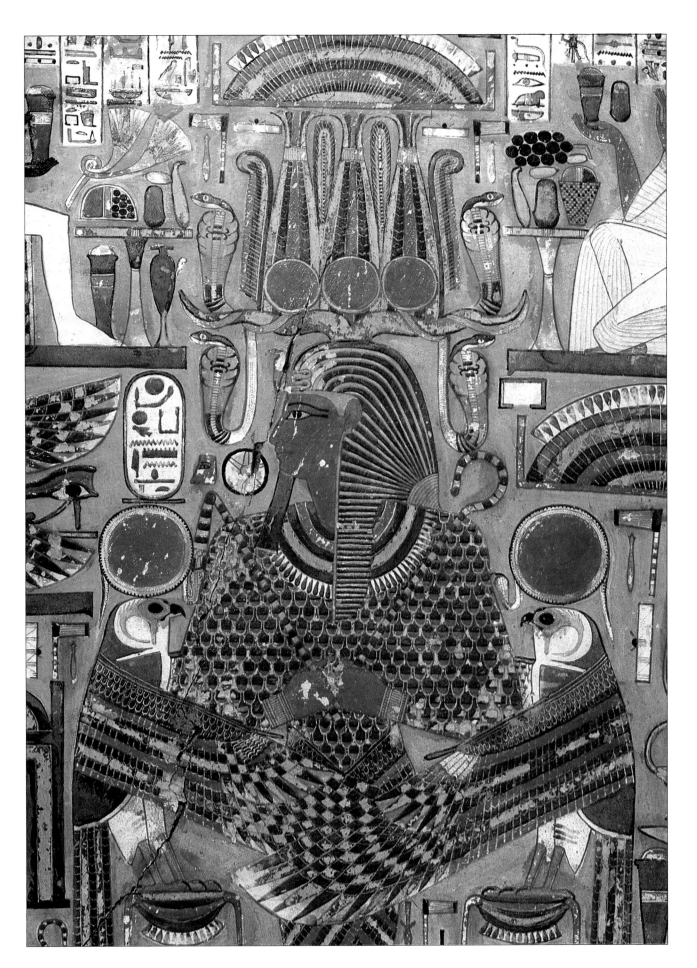

ABOVE LEFT: *Painted wooden figure of Osiris which would have contained a rolled papyrus of the* Book of the Dead; *c 1,300 BC. (British Museum.)*

ABOVE RIGHT: *Silver and gold figure of the god Amen Ra; c 900 BC. (British Museum.)*

The god of the morning sun was Khepri who was identified with the beetle. The scarab-beetle was thought to have created itself from its own matter as the sun seemed to create itself each morning.

The sun is usually visible in the sky over Egypt and it is not surprising that it came to be worshipped. Towards the end of the eighteenth dynasty (c1280 BC) there was a religious revolution in Egypt initiated by King Amen-hotep IV, better known as Akhenaten. This new religion was based on the worship of the sun as the exclusive source of all life and creation whose power was visible in the life-giving rays of the sun-disk called the Aten. Akhenaten claimed to be the sole agent or high priest of the Aten on earth which gave him the right to disperse local priesthoods and close the temples of rival deities. The

temples built for the worship of the Aten were architecturally different from the usual type, being open to the sky and without a sanctuary for a divine statue. It was Amen-hotep III, Akhenaten's father, who first brought Aten worship to prominence but Akhenaten ordered the complete exclusion of all the other gods. However, after Akhena-ten's death the old gods were reinstated at Thebes and Akhenaten was regarded as a heretic.

An essential part of Egyptian religion was the belief in life after death and the final judge-ment of the individual soul. The god Osiris was both king of the dead and judge of the underworld. In Egyptian mythology Osiris was a good Pharaoh, who was murdered by his evil brother Seth, and his death was avenged by his son, Horus. Osiris was even-

ABOVE: *Khepri the scarab-
beetle god, from a painted
coffin c 1,050 BC. (British
Museum.)*

BELOW: *King Akhenaten
and Queen Nefertiti with
their children. Above them
is the sun disc with the rays
of the sun symbolizing the
god Aten which they
worshipped.*

tually brought back to life, not as a human Pharaoh but as mummiform king of the underworld. Osiris had an important quality that made him more popular than the other gods. As a human king, he had experienced death and had triumphed over it and could assure his followers an eternal life. It was believed that every king would become Osiris after he died while his successor was the embodiment of Horus, his son. By the Middle Kingdom (c2000 BC), all worshippers of Osiris could themselves look forward to becoming an Osiris when they died and would thereby enjoy eternal life. Abydos was one of the major centres of Osiris worship and many Egyptians left inscriptions and offerings there to the god. Here they could witness the annual drama enacting the death and resurrection of Osiris, most of which took place outdoors.

Osiris was also a god of vegetation which may have been his original role. He embodied the yearly cycle of the renewal or rebirth of the land of Egypt after the Nile floods. His resurrection as king of the dead and this renewal as a vegetation god were closely linked. The wife of Osiris, Isis, represented the devoted wife and loving mother and was a very pop-

ABOVE LEFT: *Glazed figure of the lioness goddess Sekhmet. (British Museum.)*

BELOW LEFT: *This gilded bronze figure of Isis and Horus provided the universal image of a mother and child. (British Museum.)*

ABOVE RIGHT: *Bronze statuette of the Ram god Knum. (British Museum.)*

LEFT: *The Jackal god, Anubis, who was the guardian of the dead – painted relief from the tomb of Horemheb c 1,320 BC.*

ular goddess of magic who continued to be worshipped in Roman times. Osiris, Isis and Horus represented a family unit and a triad of gods. Similar groupings of three existed among many other Egyptian gods. The most notable other triads of gods were worshipped at Thebes (Amun, Mut and Khons) and Memphis (Ptah, Sekhmet and Nefertum). Osiris received general acceptance throughout Egypt and was not only a state god but also a popular god to whom ordinary people could relate.

Many other gods protected ordinary Egyptians who worshipped them in their houses. Some of the gods had no temples dedicated to them or had no place in the official temple rituals. One of the most popular of these minor gods was Bes, who was depicted as a homely, ugly dwarf god. Bes was regarded as a bringer of joy who warded off evil spirits and protected women in childbirth. The hippopotamus goddess Tauret also protected pregnant women, as did the cat goddess Bastet and the cow goddess Hathor, who were also associated with dancing and music. Representations of these household gods were used as decorative elements in the finer everyday items of the wealthy, such as beds, headrests, mirrors and cosmetic pots. Images of the gods were thought to have supernatural powers and the Egyptians wore many amulets to protect themselves. Many small faience charms were placed with their

mummies to protect them on their hazardous journey to the next world and their tombs contained models, statues and paintings which had a similar magical role.

It is impossible to arrange Ancient Egyptian gods into neat categories since their religious ideas were very complex. The sheer number of gods is staggering since their religion developed over a very long period of time and they did not discard old beliefs when new ones became popular. From the earliest times, there were local tribal gods in various regions of the country and some of these rose to great prominence during various periods of history. Often for political reasons, many gods were also combined together as a means of consolidating their special powers.

The belief in a divine power, as an indeterminate and impersonal force universally present in all their gods, was an essential part of Egyptian religious thought. Before gods had a particular form or were given a name the Egyptians would have worshipped the abstract concept of power. Their belief in the supernatural was closely interwoven with their daily lives, their personal relationships, their hopes and fears and their attitude to the Pharaoh's supreme authority. The day-to-day hazards of existence were believed to be the work of hostile powers which could be suppressed by maintaining religious cults and preserving a divine order.

CHAPTER FIVE

The
MUMMIES

ABOVE: *Painted
wooden coffin and mummy
of a Theban priestess, c
1,000 BC. (British
Museum.)*

Mummies are the first things most people think about at the mention of Ancient Egypt, but what exactly are they and how and why were they made? Although the term 'mummy' is associated with Ancient Egypt, it is also applied to preserved bodies from many other cultures. The word itself comes from the Arabic name for 'bitumen', and was used to describe these bodies because their black appearance suggested that they had been coated in pitch. Most of the bandaged mummies that have survived date from the New Kingdom or the later half of Egyptian history. By this time, the embalming process, which had previously been reserved for royalty, became available to all who could afford it.

Why did they go to so much expense and trouble to preserve their dead? The answer is, because they believed that the survival of the body was essential for the soul to become immortal. Life after death was thought to be a re-creation of the best moments of earthly existence and so bodies were buried with their favourite possessions, a supply of food and even model labourers to do their work for them. There was nothing morbid in this life-long preoccupation with death, and gaily painted mummy cases reflect an optimism and confidence in eternal life.

The Ancient Egyptian belief in an afterlife and the development of embalming are thought to have arisen partly in response to the survival of many naturally preserved bodies from the earliest times in Egypt. In this predynastic period, the naked body was simply buried in a shallow grave in the desert.

ABOVE RIGHT: *Gilded
wooden inner coffin of a
Theban priestess, c 1,290
BC. (British Museum.)*

RIGHT: *Wooden
shabti figure of King
Amenhotep III. These
figures were placed in tombs
to carry out agricultural
work for the deceased in the
afterlife. (British
Museum.)*

ABOVE: *Head of a
male mummy with an inlaid
eye, c 1,000 BC. (British
Museum.)*

The hot, dry sand quickly absorbed the moisture from the body and prevented decay. Some of these corpses must have been exposed by grave robbers or by shifting sands, and their discovery may have inspired later generations to believe in an afterlife. As time passed, this belief led to the need for a more dignified burial which was accompanied by an increasing amount of provisions for the next life. The tomb replaced the simple grave, but this allowed the body to come into contact with the air and decompose. From the early sand burials they must have realized that the best way of preserving a body was to dehydrate it, which prevented bacteria from breeding and causing decay.

There was a ready supply of natural sodium salts to be found in Egypt, called natron, which are an effective drying agent and mildly antiseptic. With the aid of natron, the Ancient Egyptians developed an elaborate technique of embalming which could take as long as 70 days. The first stage of this process was to remove all the internal organs except the heart. (This was left since it was thought to be the centre of human intelligence which would be required for judgement in the under-

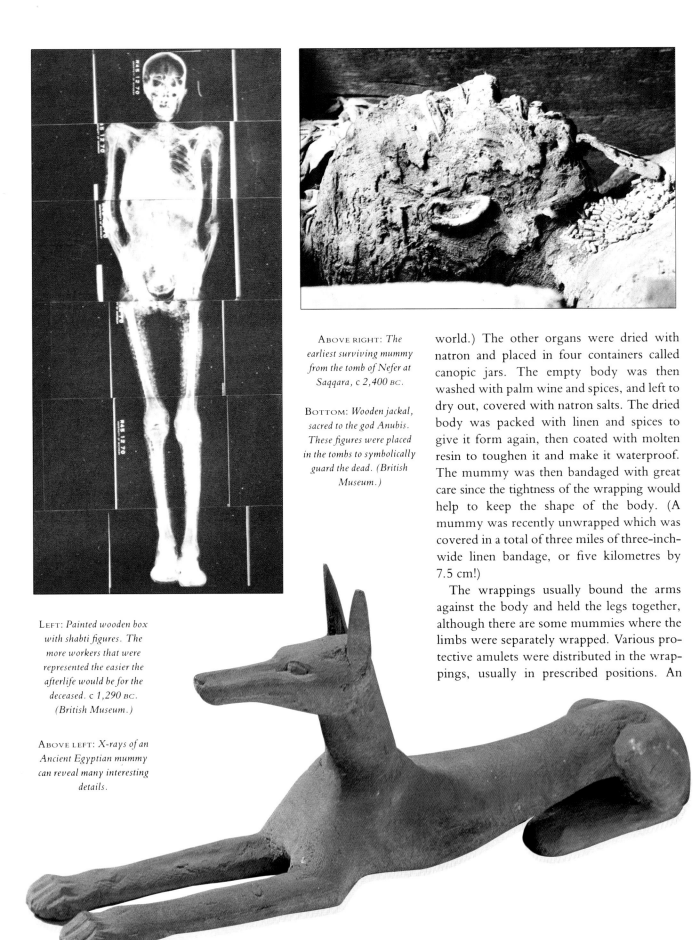

ABOVE RIGHT: *The earliest surviving mummy from the tomb of Nefer at Saqqara, c 2,400 BC.*

BOTTOM: *Wooden jackal, sacred to the god Anubis. These figures were placed in the tombs to symbolically guard the dead. (British Museum.)*

LEFT: *Painted wooden box with shabti figures. The more workers that were represented the easier the afterlife would be for the deceased. c 1,290 BC. (British Museum.)*

ABOVE LEFT: *X-rays of an Ancient Egyptian mummy can reveal many interesting details.*

world.) The other organs were dried with natron and placed in four containers called canopic jars. The empty body was then washed with palm wine and spices, and left to dry out, covered with natron salts. The dried body was packed with linen and spices to give it form again, then coated with molten resin to toughen it and make it waterproof. The mummy was then bandaged with great care since the tightness of the wrapping would help to keep the shape of the body. (A mummy was recently unwrapped which was covered in a total of three miles of three-inch-wide linen bandage, or five kilometres by 7.5 cm!)

The wrappings usually bound the arms against the body and held the legs together, although there are some mummies where the limbs were separately wrapped. Various protective amulets were distributed in the wrappings, usually in prescribed positions. An

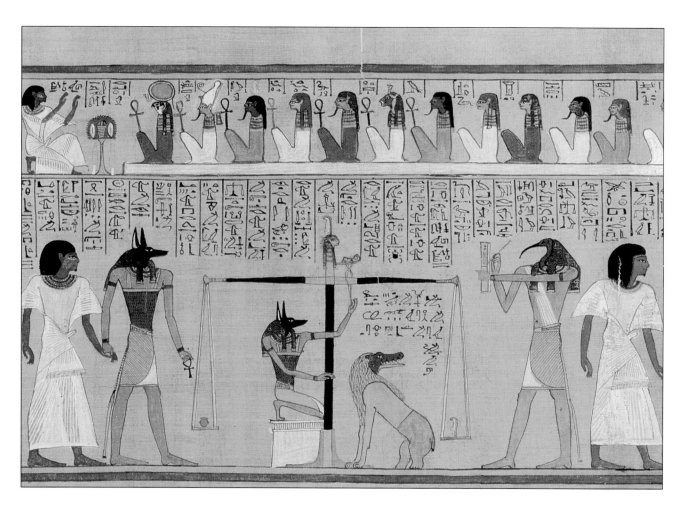

important amulet was the heart scarab, which was placed on the chest of the mummy. It was inscribed with a religious text instructing the person's heart not to make trouble for them when weighed in the judgement before Osiris. Another popular protective amulet was the eye of Horus or 'udjat' which represented the eye of a falcon, with its characteristic markings beneath.

Although the basic function of the coffin was to protect the body from violation by animals and thieves, it was also regarded as the house of the spirit. Through the magical powers of its decoration and inscriptions it could ensure the welfare of the deceased in the afterlife. The coffin underwent various changes in shape, material and decoration throughout the long period of Ancient Egyptian history. Some of the earliest coffins were small and made of clay, basketwork or wood where the body lay in a hunched up position on its side. In the Middle Kingdom (c2000 BC) full-length double wooden coffins were often provided. The inner one could be made in the shape of the mummy, while the outer coffin was rectangular. On the inside

ABOVE: Scene showing the weighing of the mummy's heart as part of the judgement in the afterlife. From the Book of the Dead *of the scribe Hunefer, c 1,310 BC. (British Museum.)*

BOTTOM: Set of limestone canopic jars for holding the internal organs of the mummy; c 1,000 BC. (British Museum.)

RIGHT: Some coffins were carved from stone, like this fine basalt example made for a vizier, c 500 BC. (British Museum.)

this rectangular coffin was decorated with personal objects and magical texts, while on the outside it had a large pair of eyes painted in a panel by the left shoulder so that the mummy inside could look out at the world. These eyes were often painted above a representation of a doorway, through which the mummy's spirit could leave at will and have access to the rest of the tomb.

The characteristic coffins in the shape of the mummified body with an idealized face mask are mostly of New Kingdom date or later. The stereotyped faces often had a false beard to symbolize their identification with

the dead King Osiris. The coffins were painted with a representation of the sky goddess Nut who spread her wings protectively over the lid, since she was traditionally the mother of the deceased who was associated with her godly son, Osiris. The coffins were usually made of thin planks of wood skilfully dowelled together, and the arms of the mummy were often shown carved in high relief and crossed over the chest. Painted bands of jewellery and floral collars reproduced the ornaments on the actual mummy. The head of the mummy was often enclosed in a mask of cartonnage – layers of linen stuck together and covered with a thin coat of plaster. This mask was often extended to cover the complete body and formed an ideal ground for elaborate decoration. Sometimes a painted and modelled board was placed over the body inside the coffin as an economical way of suggesting a double coffin.

In the saite period (after 600 BC) some superb hard stone mummyform coffins were made and the mummy was often covered in a bead net. By the late period many corpses were not even properly embalmed, being simply painted with pitch and wrapped with bandages. Although the vital organs were often left in the body, 'dummy' canopic jars were still provided for them which had a purely symbolic function. By Graeco-Roman times the idealized face mask was often replaced with a more realistic portrait painted on a wooden panel while the bandages were arranged in intricate geometric patterns.

Few royal coffins have survived but the evidence is that they were of gilded wood, inlaid with stones and glass paste. Surviving intact examples are the three-nested coffins of Tutankhamun. They were enclosed in a rectangular stone sarcophagus decorated inside and out with funeral gods in painted relief. One of the finest stone sarcophagi is that of King Seti I, which is of white calcite inlaid with rows of funerary figures in blue paste. The kings of the 21st and 22nd dynasties from Tanis (c950 BC) were buried in mummiform coffins of silver and gilded wood, two of them with silver hawks' heads.

The mummy's eternal dwelling place was the tomb. The type of tomb varied according to the period, the area and the owner's social status. We should not forget that the vast majority of poor Ancient Egyptians would have had a simple burial in the desert with

ABOVE: *Elaborately bandaged mummy of a calf, c 30 BC. The Egyptians mummified many of their sacred animals. (British Museum.)*

BOTTOM: *A finely carved wooden face from a coffin with inlaid eyes of lapis lazuli and glass. (British Museum.)*

LEFT: *Gilded mummy mask made from cartonnage, a material composed of linen or papyrus coated in plaster. (British Museum.)*

few possessions. The tombs of the privileged who could afford a more elaborate burial were either built of stone and brick or cut out of the solid rock. They all generally consist of two main parts, the burial chamber and the funerary chapel. The Old Kingdom tombs had a false door which served as a magical entrance through which the spirit of the deceased could pass from the burial chamber on the western side of the tomb into the chapel on the east. Here the spirit could partake of the offerings of food and drink provided by the relatives or priests. In the carved reliefs on the walls of the tomb, scenes of farming, hunting, fishing, baking and brewing ensured that provisions for the deceased would be continually available. As time went on these were supplemented by representational models and a large variety of personal possessions. The royal tombs in the Valley of the Kings at Thebes were completely closed with entrance stairs to four passages or corridors, a hall and a burial chamber. These all had a symbolic significance in the journey of the spirit in the afterlife.

This journey of the spirit is recorded in detail on papyri which were often placed in tombs from the New Kingdom onwards. These religious writings are known as Books of the Dead which were copies of earlier Old

ABOVE: *The tomb of Queen Nefertari, wife of Ramses II, is probably the most beautifully painted Ancient Egyptian tomb; c 1,250 BC.*

Kingdom stone inscriptions called the Pyramid Texts. The principal magical function of these writings was to secure for the deceased a satisfactory afterlife and to give him the power to leave his tomb when necessary. They include painted depictions of Anubis the god of mummification and show the final judgement before Osiris, the king of the dead. The mummy's personality or spirit is identified with the Ba-Bird which is portrayed as a human-headed bird hovering over the mummy.

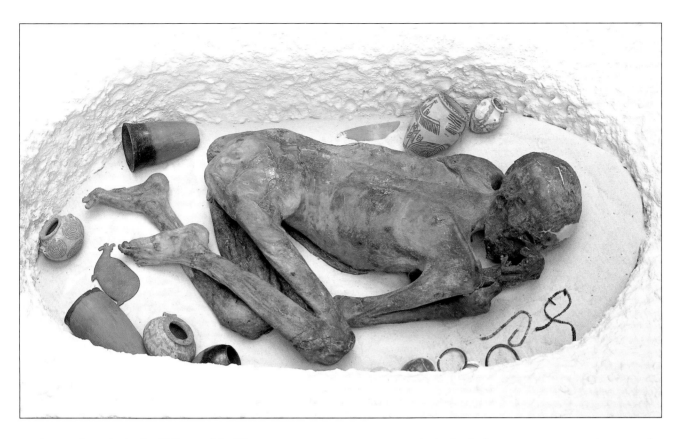

The royal tombs in the Valleys of the Kings and Queens at Thebes, were located continuously in ancient times. In order to prevent further violation, the mummies were removed secretly by the Theban priests and most of them were hidden in a deep shaft in the cliff face. Although they were eventually discovered by local villagers in the last century, who began to profit from the discovery, they were rescued by the Egyptian Antiquities Service. When they were finally transported to Cairo for the museum in 1881, the customs officer at the city gates levied a duty on them, classifying them as dried fish!

Most of the hundreds of mummies distributed throughout the world in museums and collections date from the late periods when entire families were buried together in communal catacombs. Richly painted religious scenes on these coffins replaced the need for individual tombs. From the time that mummies acquired a market value, these tombs, where the mummies were stacked, were ransacked by villagers living near the Theban cemeteries. In the sixteenth century mummies were thought to have special healing properties and many were ground up to make medicines. In order to meet the rising demand for this thriving business, fake mummies were produced using the corpses of executed crim-

ABOVE LEFT: Wooden coffin decorated with bands of inscription which include a prayer for food offerings. At the head end, two painted eyes enable the mummy to see out above a painted false door through which his spirit could pass. c 2,000 BC. (British Museum.)

ABOVE: The body of a man preserved naturally by the hot dry sand in which he was buried. The heat of the sand absorbed the moisture without which bacteria cannot breed and cause decay. Ironically this humble form of burial preserved the body far better than the most elaborate tombs and costly embalming techniques. c 3,200 BC. (British Museum.)

inals. In the last century, mummies were also ground up to be used as a brown artists' pigment and sold in tubes labelled 'mummy'. The Ancient Egyptians also mummified all manner of sacred animals, which were placed in special sanctuaries beneath temples and vast quantities of these have survived. At the turn of the century some 300,000 cat mummies were shipped to Liverpool, to be turned into fertilizer and sold for £4 ($7) a ton!

The unwrapping and autopsy of mummies in various institutions continues to be carried out by leading medical specialists using the latest techniques and equipment. Powerful electron microscopes, forensic tests and x-rays can often reveal the diseases that the Ancient Egyptians suffered from, their cause of death and their diet. Examination of the teeth of mummies can indicate what foods they ate and there is evidence that they practised dentistry. Some teeth have been found to contain a form of mineral cement or have been bound together with fine gold wire. By detecting blood groups and hereditary traits from royal mummies it is also possible to identify particular family connections. Establishing the age of certain kings at the time of death can also help specialists to verify the dates of various dynasties or important events in Egyptian history.

CHAPTER SIX

EGYPTIAN LIFE

ABOVE: *Painted wooden model of a woman carrying a tray of cakes. (British Museum.)*

Much can be learnt about Ancient Egyptian life from the everyday items and wall-paintings to be found in their tombs. They believed that these representations of work and pleasure would assist them in the afterlife. Many tombs and temples have survived from ancient times because they were made of stone. Few houses remain since they were built from perishable materials, like mud-brick which collapsed when it was old, and is now used as a fertilizer. Many towns and villages continued to be inhabited throughout history until modern times and houses were frequently rebuilt and the material recycled. Many modern Egyptian villages probably resemble the ancient ones quite closely in their construction and way of life. Occasionally, settlements were completely abandoned, and excavating them can tell us a great deal about the daily life of the ordinary people. The two most notable sites of this kind are King Akhenaten's city at El-Amarna and the village of the workmen who built the tombs in the Valley of the Kings at Deir el-Medina. This village grew over four centuries. Rectangular walls originally enclosed the streets and houses which were laid out in a regular pattern. The individual houses were roughly the same size except for the larger houses of the foremen.

A typical house had three main rooms, with a yard, which acted as a kitchen, and two cellars for storage. There were often niches set into the walls for religious stone inscriptions, images of household gods or busts of family ancestors. Many houses came to be modified to suit individual needs or activities and some included work-rooms and shops. At El-Amarna, the finer houses had two floors and basement store rooms. They might also have a reception hall, kitchen and servants' quarters, while some even had bathrooms and lavatories. A number of walled houses had an enclosed garden with a fish pond and shady trees. Furniture consisted of beds, small tables, stools and wooden storage chests for utensils and jewellery. Hangings, mats and textiles decorated the inner rooms. Like many African peoples, the Egyptians used headrests instead of pillows for sleeping on. Many of these have survived made from either wood, ivory or stone, and they consist of a curved neckpiece set on top of a pillar which sits on an oblong base. They had lamps which were simple bowls of pottery or

ABOVE: *From a wall painting in a Theban tomb showing jewellers and carpenters at work.*

stone containing oil and a wick. They also used pottery torches which could be set into brackets on the wall. Kitchens and cellars had clay ovens and large storage jars for wine, oil and grain.

The workmen who lived at Deir el-Medina were stonemasons, plasterers, sculptors, draughtsmen, painters and carpenters. The valley contains the remains of their houses, tombs, chapels, rest houses and domestic rubbish. Many written documents have been discovered there which deal with the progress of the work and there is even the earliest record of a strike when there was a delay in paying their wages. The men would have worked for eight days out of ten living in huts above the Valley of the Kings and returning to the village for their two days of rest. Attendance registers have survived and we know that absenteeism was common. Days were lost through brewing beer, drinking, and building houses, and there were also many religious holidays. Their wages were paid in wheat, fish, vegetables, cosmetic oils, wood for fuel, pottery and clothing. They used each other's skills to construct highly decorated tombs for themselves and there were many opportunities to undertake private commissions from wealthy Thebans.

Many legal documents have survived from Deir el-Medina concerning crimes and judgements, inheritances, and business transactions. The Ancient Egyptians had a legal system of courts and magistrates and they had a wide range of punishments which included forced labour camps. They had a type of police force, distinct from the army, who often used trained dogs. There existed a system of giving evidence under oath and documents often contain signatures of witnesses. Documents were legalized by affixing a seal and deposited at a record office or temple. The Ancient Egyptians had schools, but these would have been for training future scribes and officials intended for the priesthood or the civil administration who were exclusively male. The royal family had special tutors, and ordinary people were educated at home. The father traditionally handed down advice and professional secrets to his son relating to his trade or craft. Craftsmen, like officials, had an apprenticeship system.

Technical skill was greatly admired but there was no distinction between artists and craftsmen and therefore art is generally anonymous. Craftsmen were employed by the king or the temple officials and their achievement and skill using simple tools is remarkable.

ABOVE: *Painted wooden model of breadmakers, c 2,000 BC. (British Museum.)*

ABOVE LEFT: *Painted wooden model of a man ploughing. (British Museum.)*

ABOVE RIGHT: *Painted wooden model of a woman carrying a tray of cakes. (British Museum.)*

Their most impressive achievements were in sculpture, both in the round and in carved relief. They also mastered the technique of making fine stone vessels from an early date. The precision of their carpentry was also very fine and wood was joined by dovetailing, mitres, mortice-and-tenon joints and dowels. Inlay and veneer were common forms of decoration and the Egyptians were the first to use plywood. Their tools, which would have been copper, included axes, saws, adzes, chisels and drills. The wood, much of which

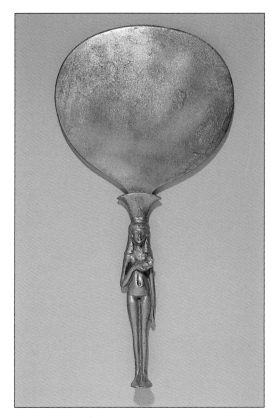

was imported, was mainly cedar, sycamore, acacia, ebony and palmwood. Metal workers and jewellers show a high degree of skill in using techniques like chasing, engraving, embossing, inlaying, filigree work and enamelling. They could beat gold into leaf as fine as 0.005 mm, and gemstones and beads of small sizes were bored with precision using a bow drill. Copper was smelted using a type of bellows and bronze was cast by the lost-wax process. These materials were essential for making tools, weapons, ritual utensils and religious statuettes.

Another characteristic Egyptian craft technique was the manufacture of glass and glazed ware. Faience ware, usually of blue-green or turquoise glaze, was produced in vast quantities, often from moulds. The Egyptians could also produce linen of outstanding quality and a shawl discovered in Tutankhamun's tomb is made of the finest linen known. Textile experts have estimated that it must have taken about 3,000 hours to make or nine months of eleven-hour days. Allied to weaving was the manufacture of mats, baskets and rope using reed, flax, papyrus, palm fibre and grass. Countless baskets and pottery have survived which were the standard household container.

The majority of the population were engaged in working on the land and their labour

was conscripted for irrigation systems or royal building projects. This conscription was for everyone, but privileged officials could avoid it by paying someone else to work on their behalf. Foreign prisoners-of-war and criminals were also used in gangs for heavier work like stone quarrying. Conscripted workers received no payment for their services, only subsistence. Even the poorest peasant labourers and domestic servants were not slaves in the usual sense of the word. All Egyptians had legal rights and could own or dispose of their possessions. There was no system of citizenship or slavery, as clearly defined in Greece and Rome. Egyptian society never produced a true middle class and the social structure was a hierarchy of officials where everyone ultimately served the Pharaoh who was the embodiment of the state.

In addition to cereals, flax was grown in great quantities, to be spun into thread and finally woven into linen. Large herds of cattle

ABOVE LEFT: *Bronze mirror which would originally have been highly polished. (British Museum.)*

ABOVE RIGHT: *Ladies' vanity box containing a selection of cosmetics vessels, toilet objects and pair of sandals. (British Museum.)*

ABOVE: *The workmen's village at Deir el-Medina.*

ABOVE LEFT: *Gold handled dagger. (British Museum.)*

ABOVE RIGHT: *A man and his wife with a tray of food offerings and wine in storage jars.*

gold, silver or copper. Payments could be made in given weights or rings of the metal itself (unlike coins, these pieces had no official markings as a guarantee of value), or commodities like produce or livestock.

The family was at the heart of Egyptian society and early marriage and parenthood were encouraged. Many marriages would have been arranged but the romantic nature of surviving love poetry suggests that there was some freedom of choice. Marriage tended to be within the same social group, and family unions between uncle and niece or cousins were common. The words 'brother' and 'sister' were often used merely as terms of endearment in their writings and have led to a misconception that the Egyptians committed

were reared and cows dragged the plough and provided milk. Other livestock kept included sheep, pigs and donkeys. Surplus agricultural produce and linen were exported by the royal government who controlled trade. In country markets barter or exchange was the means of trade. The Ancient Egyptians managed without coinage during their long history. They had a system of valuing provisions and manufactured articles in various units equivalent to fixed amounts of

LEFT: *A finely carved limestone statue of a man and his wife, showing the complexity of their wigs. (British Museum.)*

BOTTOM LEFT: *Painted limestone statue of a seated woman showing a typical style of dress. (British Museum.)*

BOTTOM RIGHT: *Blue-glazed drinking-cup in the form of a lotus. (British Museum.)*

incest. There was no religious or civil marriage ceremony although there were family parties and festivities to celebrate the occasion. Marriage was a private legal agreement, and a contract established the right of both parties to maintenance and possessions. There was consequently an equality between men and women in their common opportunity to own, manage and receive property. If there was a divorce, the rights of the wife were protected equally with those of her husband. In some periods of Egyptian history even a woman who committed adultery still had certain rights to maintenance from her former husband. In spite of the formal legal contract of marriage with the facility for divorce, marriages were not usually short-lived or lacking in affection. Many statues and wall-paintings show married couples displaying gestures of affection for each other and their surviving literature often suggests sincere emotional ties.

Many tomb paintings depict large feasts of food which had a magical function and give a misleading impression that they had endless supplies of surplus food. The average Egyptian peasant probably lived on a few rolls of bread, a pot of beer and some onions. The staple food was always bread and by the time of the

ABOVE: Group of female musicians playing a harp, lute, flutes and lyre.

ABOVE LEFT: Man picking grapes to make wine; from a Theban tomb painting.

BELOW LEFT: Wooden box inlaid with coloured ivory and a selection of typical Egyptian jewellery and amulets. (British Museum.)

New Kingdom there were as many as 40 different varieties. The shapes of the loaves varied: some were oval, some round while others were conical. Different flours and honey, milk and eggs were sometimes added. Meat included beef, goat, mutton, pork, goose and pigeon. However, meat would not keep in the hot climate and had to be consumed rapidly, so for most people it would only be eaten on religious feast days. Fish was eaten more frequently particularly among the people living around the marshes.

Besides the cereals from which bread was made, farming provided many varieties of vegetables which included leeks, onions, garlic and cucumbers. Figs, dates, pomegranates and grapes were among the quantities of fruit available. Farms provided milk and milk products and they hatched eggs artificially. Honey played a large part in their diet as a sugar substitute and it was produced from bee-keeping. Beer was the most popular drink and it was prepared from barley which was ground and kneaded to make a dough and lightly baked like bread. This bread was then soaked in water, perhaps with the addition of dates for sweetening. After fermenting, the liquid was strained from the dough into a pot. They also made wine and various

regions were noted for their quality. It was stored in pottery jars and had a label noting its origin, maker and date. There were many accounts of drunkenness especially after excessive banquets and parties.

We know a lot about the clothing the Ancient Egyptians wore since it is depicted in countless sculptures and paintings. Many examples of the actual clothing have also been discovered amongst other tomb artefacts. A large number of textiles were found in Tutankhamun's tomb which included over a hundred loin cloths and about 30 gloves or chariot driving gauntlets. The world's earliest surviving dress made of stitched linen, was discovered at Tarkhan in Egypt and dates from 2,800 BC. White linen was the standard material for clothing as it was cool and light to wear. Garments were often carefully pleated and they were draped around the body rather than tailored, with minimum stitching. Simple ankle-length sheath dresses were worn. In the New Kingdom they were often more pleated and fringes became popular. Women also sometimes wore an elegant heavily pleated, fringed robe over this dress. Men usually wore a short kilt, made from a rectangular piece of linen folded round the body and tied or fastened at the waist. This was sometimes starched at the front to form an apron, or pleated. Occasionally they would wear a cloak in the cooler weather. Working men wore only a loincloth while children are often depicted naked. The wealthy had a type of laundry service with meticulous methods of washing and pleating, and numerous laundry lists and marks on clothing have survived. Sandals were worn made from woven reed, grass or leather sometimes upturned like Turkish slippers.

Elaborate and colourful jewellery contrasted well with the usually plain garments. Jewellery was worn both for personal adornment and as a protection against evil. The most characteristic form of jewellery was the collar which was composed of numerous strings of beads using attractive stones like carnelian, jaspar and lapis lazuli. Armlets, bracelets and anklets were worn while finger rings often included seals. In the New Kingdom, both men and women had pierced ears and a wide variety of earrings and ear studs survive. There are many hairstyles depicted in sculpture and wall-paintings with fashions varying according to the period. Men usually wore a rounded hairstyle that followed the line of their heads. They were generally clean-shaven and razors were used from the earliest times in Egypt. The priests shaved their heads as did the wealthier men and women who wore wigs. These were mainly of human hair with some vegetable-fibre padding. Some wigs have survived that are composed of an intricate assortment of curls and plaits sometimes with attached bead ornaments.

The Egyptians were very fond of cosmetics and men, women and children used facial make-up called kohl to create a dark line round the eyes. Besides being decorative, kohl protected the eyes against infection and stopped the glare of the sun. Red ochre was used to colour the cheeks and probably as lipstick, while henna was used as a hair colourant. Countless bronze mirrors have survived (which would originally have been highly polished) and a large variety of cosmetic vessels, spoons and applicators. Medical papyri mention recipes for creams and oils to keep

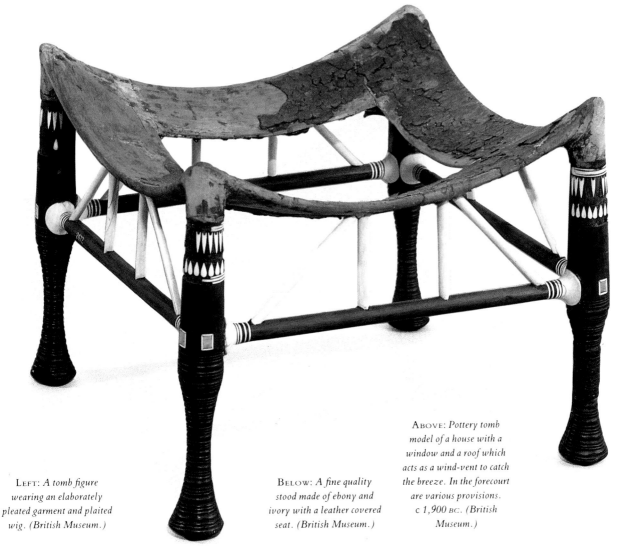

LEFT: *A tomb figure wearing an elaborately pleated garment and plaited wig. (British Museum.)*

BELOW: *A fine quality stood made of ebony and ivory with a leather covered seat. (British Museum.)*

ABOVE: *Pottery tomb model of a house with a window and a roof which acts as a wind-vent to catch the breeze. In the forecourt are various provisions. c 1,900 BC. (British Museum.)*

73

ABOVE: *A banquet scene with musicians and dancers and jars of wine. On their heads the women wear incense cones to perfume their wigs and garments. From a Theban tomb painting; c 1,400 BC. (British Museum.)*

BELOW: *A man and his wife playing the board game senet – from a papyrus, c 1,250 BC. (British Museum.)*

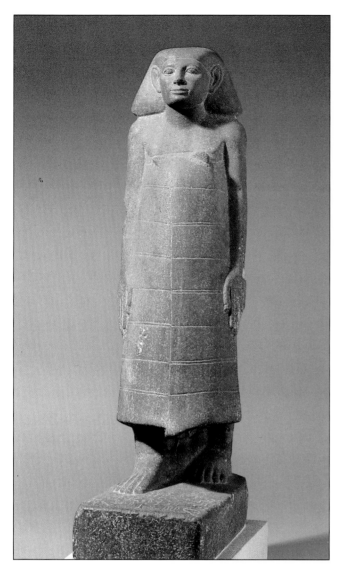

the skin soft and supple after exposure to the hot Egyptian sun. Perfumes, some of which took months to prepare, were popular and were also worn by men during certain festivals. A popular form of incense cone was worn by women on top of the head at banquets to perfume the wig and garments.

The Egyptians depicted many of their favourite pastimes in their tombs because they wanted to enjoy them forever in the afterlife. Hunting was popular among the nobility and the wealthy. Athletic games and sports were often group activities and these included wrestling, boxing, stave-fighting, ball games, gymnastics and acrobatics. Many paintings have survived of banqueting scenes where acrobats and dancers performed. The pirouette and some other ballet movements were known to the Ancient Egyptians, and dancing with rhythmic accompaniment from clapping, cymbals, sistra, bells and chanting

ABOVE LEFT: Woman wearing a dress of the style worn by officials and dignitaries at the end of the Middle Kingdom. This statue is carved from quartzite, one of the hardest stones to be worked by the Egyptians. (British Museum.)

ABOVE RIGHT: A man with food offerings which include a goat, a hare and tray of ostrich eggs.

was also popular at religious festivals. Music was an essential accompaniment to dance but was also practised in its own right. The harp and the flute were used, together with various wind instruments with and without reeds, made from wood or metal. Probably the earliest known account of a full orchestra performing a concert dates from *c*250 BC. This was at a festival for the Pharaoh Ptolemy II, where 600 musicians played simultaneously.

The Egyptians also played board games. The most popular game was called 'Senet' and many highly decorative boards with counters have survived, usually made of wood and ivory. Some boards have an alternative game on the other side which was called 'Twenty Squares'. There were also games called 'Serpent' and 'Dog and the Jackal'. Children amused themselves with a variety of toys which included balls, tops, dolls and figures of animals with movable parts.

CHAPTER SEVEN

The
NILE

ABOVE: *Sunset on the Nile.*

The Nile flows for over 4,000 miles (6,500 km) and is the longest river in the World. It is formed from two great streams, the Blue Nile, which rises in Ethiopia, and the White Nile, which rises in Uganda. They join at Khartoum to become the main river which runs north through the desert to the Mediterranean Sea. Along its course the river is interrupted at six points by rapids or cataracts, and the first of these, near Aswan, marks the Nile's entry into Egypt proper. For the last hundred odd miles (160 km), the river fans out in tributaries over the marshy flats of the delta. This northern region of Egypt, which includes the Delta, is known as Lower Egypt. The part to the south of it, called Upper Egypt, is quite different geographically. Here the land is drier and the river is bordered on both sides by cliffs.

Every year the main stream of the Nile, charged with torrential Ethiopian rainfall, traditionally distributed its water over Egypt. When the water receded it left behind a layer of fertile silt. The Ancient Egyptians called this the 'black land' to distinguish it from the 'red land' of the desert. The Nile gave them prosperity as the desert that it runs through provided security and protection from invasion. The contrast between these two geographical features affected the mental attitudes of the people who depended on them. They believed that the Nile was the centre of the world and the most important highway separating east from west. In the cycle of the Nile flood they could sense the continuity of life. By contrast, the desert was considered the home of the dead and a place for burial. Since the sun went down in the west, the desolate desert areas on the west bank were chosen for building their cemeteries. In Egyptian mythology the Nile was like the River Styx of the Greeks, where the soul was ferried from the east to west bank. In their creation mythology, the first living matter could be likened to the fresh land deposited after the flood. The Egyptians called their country 'the gift of the Nile' and the annual flood was seen as the arrival of the Nile god, Hapy.

If the annual flood of the Nile was too high, the spreading river could destroy the surrounding villages. If it was too low there was less agricultural land available for food crops. If this low flood was repeated for several consecutive years, famine resulted. The Nile made the Egyptians from the start an

ABOVE: *Fowling in the marshes – from a Theban tomb painting, c 1,400 BC.*

BELOW: *The River Temple of Philae.*

agricultural nation, and their need to organize themselves around the river's yearly cycle was crucial to the growth of their civilization. From the earliest times they managed to determine the seasons of the year by the behaviour of the Nile and developed the first working calendar of 365 days divided into 12 months. They had three seasons called 'akhet', 'peret' and 'shemu'. The season of inundation (akhet) began around August, and by November the water had receded enough to plant crops. The final season of 'shemu'

represented the drought which lasted from about March to August when the crops could be harvested.

They built dykes to prevent the river from flooding the settlements on the mounds which stood out like islands when the Nile flooded the valley. They also laid out a network of reservoirs and canals to contain the water when the flood receded. This was difficult work and the land had to be reclaimed by levelling the mounds and filling up the depressions in the ground. The water was

ABOVE: *Geese from a wall painting at Maidum, c 2,500 BC.*

MIDDLE: *Sunset on the Nile.*

BOTTOM: *After the construction of the Aswan High Dam, the River Temple of Philae had to be moved to another island – an amazing feat of organisation.*

directed into artificial canals which ran through the provincial settlements. These canals had to be dug and cleared and the courses planned to irrigate evenly as many fields as possisble. The flood water contained in reservoirs or large dug-out basins was fed into irrigation channels by simple, yet effective water-raising mechanisms. The introduction of the 'shaduf' in the New Kingdom greatly lightened the labour and is still used in Egypt nowadays. The shaduf consisted of a bucket on a pole, which was lowered into the water and then raised again by a heavy counterweight on the other end of the pole. At the end of the summer, holes were made in the dykes at the highest points, and when the required amount of muddy water had flowed through the opening was plugged. When the water had been absorbed, work could begin and the seed was sown.

The building and maintenance of the dykes, reservoirs and canals went on continuously and demanded a large labour force which was enrolled by a conscription system. (In the Old Kingdom this large organized labour force could undertake pyramid building during the inundation season.) In order to ensure the development of irrigation and land reclamation Egypt was divided into a number of administrative provinces called 'names'. When there was political crisis, the maintenance of the system of water supply became disorganized and in a short time the complete

ABOVE: *Fishing on the Nile with a draw net, from a Theban tomb painting; c 1,250 BC.*

MIDDLE: *Model boat under sail. On the prow a man tests the depth of the water while the large oar is used for steering. c 1,800 BC. (British Museum.)*

BELOW: *Colourful glass fish used as a cosmetic vessel; c1,800 BC. (British Museum.)*

economy of the country would break down. In a land of virtually no rain, irrigation alone made it possible for crops to grow and people to live. In order to help combat the consequences of a poor flood, grain could be stored up against a bad year or succession of bad years, as in the biblical story of Joseph. They also built gauges to measure the rise of the river and eventually sited these 'Nilometers' further south in order to predict the economic repercussions as early as possible.

The Nile also formed a perfect artery of communication and, unlike transport by land, it was cheap and quick, since all the cities and

TOP: *Ship under full sail from a Theban tomb painting; c2,250 BC.*

ABOVE: *Transporting cattle by boat; from a Theban tomb painting.*

RIGHT: *Black granite statue of Hapy, god of the abundant Nile. (British Museum.)*

towns were easily accessible by boat. Even allowing for all hazards, the Nile is not a particularly formidable river, and nowadays the main leisurely tours of Egypt are on cruise-boats. All the necessary water power is provided by the current and the wind. The current can provide enough power to drift down-river, while the wind blowing from the north can be harnessed to sail upstream. The earliest record of a ship under sail is depicted on an Egyptian pot which dates from about 3,200 BC. The Egyptians pioneered the development of river craft and there were

ABOVE: *In ancient times, the Nile was the natural habitat of the hippopotamus. Although associated with the gods, this creature was also hunted with harpoons.*

LEFT: *Model funeral boat which would have carried the deceased on their final journey on the Nile to their tomb; c 1,900 BC. [British Museum.]*

many different types built for various functions. Agricultural produce, troops, cattle, wood, stone and funeral processions were all carried on the Nile and its canals. The dockyards could launch ships some 200 feet (70 m) long, made of either native wood or conifers from Lebanon. Complete ships, models, detailed drawings and a technical vocabulary specifying the various types of boat, with lists of their equipment, have survived. The Ancient Egyptian language itself contains many nautical metaphors and going south was expressed as 'going upstream'.

The land around the Nile delta was particularly fertile and the marshland was teeming with wild life. Large areas of the marsh came to be carefully preserved for hunting, cattle-raising, wild fruits and fishing. Fishing was a prosperous occupation and those who lived on the edge of the marshes were organized into

ABOVE: *Papyrus painting showing the harvesting of flax from which linen was made; c 1,350 BC. (British Museum.)*

teams for fishing. The most effective method was to drag a great trawl-net between two boats and bring it to the bank. However, some fish were the sacred animals of certain local districts where it was forbidden to eat them. The Egyptians were probably the first to regard fishing as a sport as well as a source of food. A sketch has survived which depicts a nobleman fishing from a tank with a rod and line. Harpooning and fowling with a throw stick were also popular sports for the wealthy.

The Nile was also the natural habitat of the hippopotamus and the crocodile and, although they both became associated with gods, the hippopotamus was hunted with harpoons. The beautiful temple at Kom Ombo was dedicated to Sobek, the crocodile god and it is recorded that in 10BC at Lake Moeris, Egyptian priests had a sacred crocodile which they tamed and fed with cakes and honey wine. Neither the hippopotamus nor the crocodile

are to be found in the Egyptian river nowadays, as they have moved further south, deep into the Sudan.

In the extensive marshy areas of the Nile, the papyrus plant rooted in the mud rose to a great height and spread in dense thickets. The papyrus reed was the raw material of Egyptian paper making. Papyrus paper was made by cutting thin strips of pith (the spongy tissue in the stem of each reed) and arranging them on a flat stone. The papyrus was then beaten with wooden mallets until natural juice, acting like glue, bound the strips together. Then single sheets were pasted into one long roll. The Egyptians are known to have used papyrus as early as the first dynasty (c3,100 BC). Papyrus became an expensive government monopoly in later times and its cultivation was eventually restricted to one particular region. Papyrus no longer grows naturally in Egypt and much of the thriving tourist trade in paintings claimed to be painted on 'papy-

ABOVE: *Papyrus painting showing a cow emerging from a thicket of papyrus which grew to a great height by the Nile. (British Museum.)*

BELOW: *Travel brochures from the 1920s. Since the major ancient sites are easily accessible from the river, the Nile Cruise has become the most leisurely and luxurious way to tour Egypt.*

LEFT: *Woman carrying papyrus – the classic flowering plant of Lower Egypt.*

RIGHT: *Pharaoh carrying a bouquet of sacred lotus flowers which symbolized rebirth and were an emblem of Upper Egypt.*

rus' is often done on a substitute paper of banana skin composition.

The Greek historian, Herodotus, claimed that the first Pharaoh, Menes, had the plain of Memphis drained, in order to build a new capital there, and thereby altered the course of the Nile. There is also evidence of an immense reservoir constructed in the Faiyum region, 66 square miles (100 sq km) in area that had vast dykes and sluices. Nowadays the colossal Aswan High Dam built between 1960 and 1970, with its own immense reservoir, has ended the traditional annual flood cycle of the River Nile. The immense reser-voir, Lake Nasser, created by the dam, sub-merged whole villages and has required the resettlement of tens of thousands of people. Many important ancient remains have been lost but over 20 monuments were rescued with assistance on an international scale. The most impressive salvage operation was at Abu Simbel, where the vast rock temples were cut into 30-ton blocks and then reassembled at an identical site above the level of the lake. Similarly, the beautiful temples of Philae were painstakingly transferred stone by stone to a nearby island, safe from the floodwaters of the Nile.

CHAPTER EIGHT

T *h e*
HIEROGLYPHS

ABOVE: *Painted
limestone statuette of a
royal scribe; c1,500 BC.
(British Museum.)*

When looking at hieroglyphs we have a natural tendency to view each sign as a representation of a letter, since our written language is dependent upon an alphabet. The idea of an alphabet is something which occurred very late in the history of writing, and the reduction of all the possible sounds and combinations to a written system of some 20 signs took mankind a long time to accomplish. Each hieroglyphic sign does not represent a letter and does not always represent a word. Besides being pictorial indications of the meaning of words (ideograms), hieroglyphic signs also convey sounds in one, two, or three consonants (phonograms). Writing based solely on picture signs would be impractical since a complete vocabulary would require thousands of signs. It would be difficult to express clearly and without ambiguity, words for things not easily pictured, and this was probably why signs with a sound value (phonograms) were also necessary. The purely pictorial signs or ideograms could be used at the end of a word to indicate that word's precise meaning – a useful system in the absence of punctuation.

Ancient Egyptian is the second oldest recorded language. Only Sumerian is believed to be slightly earlier. The first hieroglyphs can be dated to approximately 3,100 BC while the latest are almost three and a half thousand years later (*c* AD 394). It could be claimed that the written language has survived in total for nearly 5,000 years since its final form is still used during Coptic religious services. A small number of Ancient Egyptian words have even found their way into the modern English vocabulary (eg 'oasis'). Egyptologists have identified five stages in the development of the language: The Old (*c*2650–2135 BC). the Middle (*c*2135–1785 BC) and Late (*c*1550–700 BC), Demotic (*c*700 BC – AD 500) and finally Coptic. This last stage began in the third century AD and continued until the Middle Ages when it was replaced by Arabic as the spoken Egyptian language.

Hieroglyphic writing was a highly developed system by which everything, even grammatical forms, could be expressed. Hieroglyphs can be read from right to left, from left to right and also vertically from top to bottom, according to the composition of the picture. A hieroglyphic inscription was traditionally arranged in columns. Later it was written in horizontal lines and the heads

of the signs were always turned towards the beginning of the sentence. The sequence is continuous, without punctuation marks or spaces to indicate divisions between words. Egyptian grammar is completely different from that of European languages and cannot be reduced to a series of simple rules. Mastery of the language takes much concerted study. There are over 6,000 documented hieroglyphs covering the whole period during which the scripts were used, although the majority of these were developed for religious reasons in the Graeco-Roman period. In general, about 700 were in standard use at any one time.

A striking feature of hieroglyphic writing is its absence of vowels. Egyptologists use the vowels 'e' and 'a' where necessary to communicate the language verbally. There are 24 hieroglyphic signs, each representing a consonant, which loosely correspond to the sounds of our modern alphabet. Egyptologists transliterate hieroglyphic sound values into our modern alphabetic characters to enable pronunciation, but the words would

ABOVE: *Papyrus with a hymn to the god Ra from the* Book of the Dead. *Hieroglyphs came to be used almost exclusively for religious and magical texts.* c 1,050 BC. *(British Museum.)*

ABOVE: *The Rosetta sto*
consists of three scripts
hieroglyphs at the top
demotic in the middle, a
Greek at the bottom. It i
decree by all the priests
Egypt in favour of the
reigning King, Ptolemy
(British Museum.)

THE ALPHABET IN HIEROGLYPHS

B
Foot

D
Hand

F
Horned Viper

G
Jar Stand

H
Aerial View of Hut

H
Twisted Flax

I
Flowering Reed

J
Similar to Snake

K
Basket

M
Owl

N
Water

P
Stool

Q
Similar to Hill Slope

R
Mouth

S
Folded Cloth

SH
Pool

T
Loaf

TSH
Tethering Rope

W
Quail Chick

Z
Similar to Door Bolt

THE NUMERICAL SYSTEM

The numbers are denoted by seven special signs

| 1   ∩ 10   100   1,000   10,000   100,000   1,000,000

When written together to form a single number the higher values are written in front of the lower values. Multiples of each are indicated by simple repetition of the sign:

7 = |||||||

369 =

24 =

142,235 =

not have sounded the same way in ancient times. This system of Egyptian alphabetic signs was not generally used for complete words until Graeco-Roman times when various royal names were transcribed into hieroglyphs. It has been claimed that certain hieroglyphs eventually found their way into our own alphabet via Protosinaitic, Phoenician, Greek and Latin.

Hieroglyphs are usually associated with stone inscriptions and the word itself is actually derived from the Greek 'ta hieroglyphica' meaning 'the sacred carved letters'. The signs of the script are largely pictorial in character and the majority of the signs are recognizable pictures of natural or manmade objects. The best examples of the script have an intrinsic beauty of line and colour which some claim to be the most beautiful writing ever designed. It was more than just a writing system and the Egyptians themselves referred to it as the 'writing of the divine words'. Like the representations in their art, the script was endowed with religious or magical significance. The name of a person inscribed in hieroglyphs was believed to embody his unique identity. If the representation lacked a name, it had no means of continued existence in the afterlife. Therefore, many kings' and gods' names

LEFT: *Painted limestone statue of a scribe in the traditional cross-legged pose with his papyrus scroll unfolded in the lap. (Cairo Museum.)*

ABOVE LEFT: *Two common carved stone hieroglyphs representing the sedge plant, symbol of Upper Egypt, and the bee symbol of Lower Egypt. (British Museum.)*

90

ABOVE: *Painted limestone relief depicting Thoth, the ibis-headed god of writing. (British Museum.)*

LEFT: *Faience book-label probably originally attached to a box of papyri in the Royal Library at El Amarna; c 1,380 BC. (British Museum.)*

BELOW: *Limestone tablet inscribed with hieroglyphs with a mallet and copper chisels. (British Museum.)*

were defaced or erased from monuments by later Pharaohs with conflicting ideals. Similarly, existing inscriptions and statues could be taken over and claimed by carving the new royal name on them.

Hieroglyphs were not suitable for writing quickly so they were developed into a more stylized, fluent script called hieratic. This became the standard administrative and business script and was also used to record documents of a literary, scientific and religious nature. It was particularly suitable for writing on papyrus or fragments of pottery and limestone called ostraca. The text was usually written with a brush or a sharpened reed in black ink, while red ink was sometimes used to highlight special sections. The name hieratic

HIEROGLYPHS

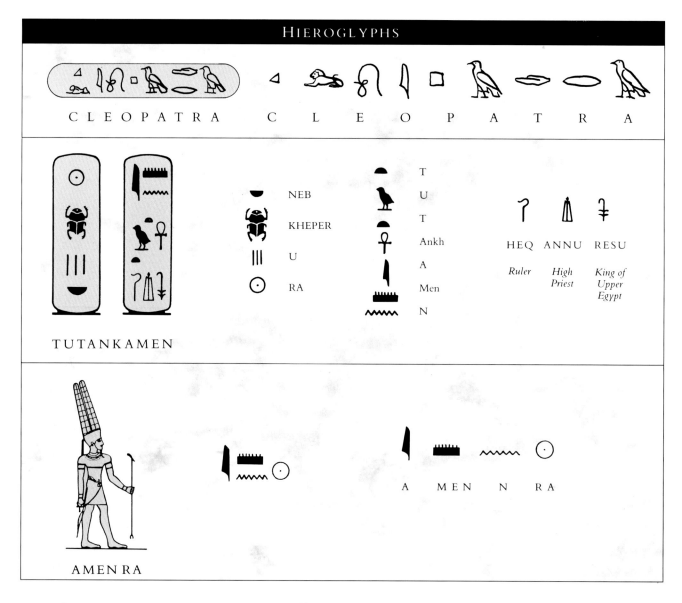

CLEOPATRA   C   L   E   O   P   A   T   R   A

TUTANKAMEN

NEB
KHEPER
U
RA

T
U
T
Ankh
A
Men
N

HEQ ANNU RESU

Ruler *High Priest* *King of Upper Egypt*

AMEN RA

A   MEN   N   RA

comes from the Greek 'hieratika' meaning 'priestly'. This was because, by the Late Period when the Greeks visited Egypt, its use had become confined to religious documents and demotic had replaced it as the main 'business' script. The name demotic comes from the Greek 'demotika' meaning 'popular' and this refers to its day-to-day writing function. From the Prolemaic period it was also used for literary compositions as well as scientific and religious texts.

Although writing played an important part in Ancient Egyptian society it is unlikely that literacy can have been widespread among the population. The production of writing and direct access to it was confined to an educated elite, consisting of royalty, state officials and scribes. The professional scribe was a central figure in every aspect of the country's administration – civil, military and religious. When an illiterate person needed a document to be read or written he would need to pay for the services of a scribe. It traditionally took a scribe some 12 years to learn and write the 700 or so hieroglyphs in common use by the New Kingdom and study started at the age of four. Many ancient school exercises have survived (complete with the teacher's corrections), and these were often copies of 'Egyptian Classics' in the hieratic text.

In Egypt's Roman and Christian period, the Coptic script developed as the other native scripts declined. The word 'copt' is derived from the Arabic 'gubti' a corruption of the Greek word for Egypt. It was used by the Arabs in the seventh century to denote the native inhabitants of the country. Coptic consists of 24 letters of the Greek alphabet combined with six demotic characters. The development of this standard form of the alphabet,

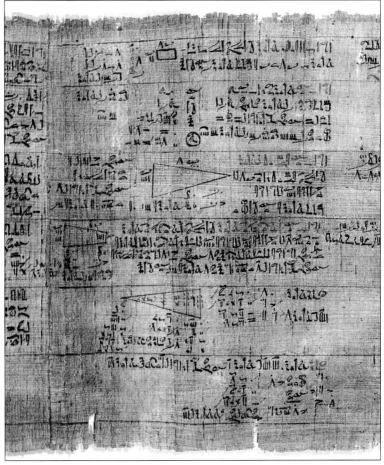

which was well established by the fourth century AD, is closely associated with the spread of Christianity in Egypt. In its earliest form, Coptic was used to write native magical texts and it was not initially devised for translating the gospels. Since it is still spoken in Coptic religious services some people believe it could reveal clues to the pronunciation of the original Ancient Egyptian language, although the links may have become too distant with the passage of time.

The art of reading hieroglyphs was lost for centuries and it was a Frenchman called Jean-Francois Champollion (1790–1832) who became the first to decipher them in full. The most important key to this forgotten writing was the famous Rosetta stone discovered in 1799 which had a bilingual text. This was a decree of the Pharaoh Prolemy V written in Ancient Greek (a known language) and two Ancient Egyptian scripts, demotic and hieroglyphic. Comparing these scripts and making use of his excellent knowledge of Coptic, Champollion studied copies of other hieroglyphic inscriptions. After considerable research he was able to recognize not only some of the letters of the hieroglyphic alphabet but also a range of other hieroglyphs from royal

LEFT: *Copy of a temple relief from Abydos showing the typical composition with its careful balance between the figures and hieroglyphs.*

ABOVE LEFT: *Faience amulet derived from the sacred eye of Horus hieroglyph. (British Museum.)*

ABOVE: *Isis greets Ramses III and his son; from a Theban tomb painting, c 1,150 BC. This shows the arrangement of columns of hieroglyphs with a pictorial composition.*

RIGHT: *Faience amulet derived from the falcon hieroglyph. (British Museum.)*

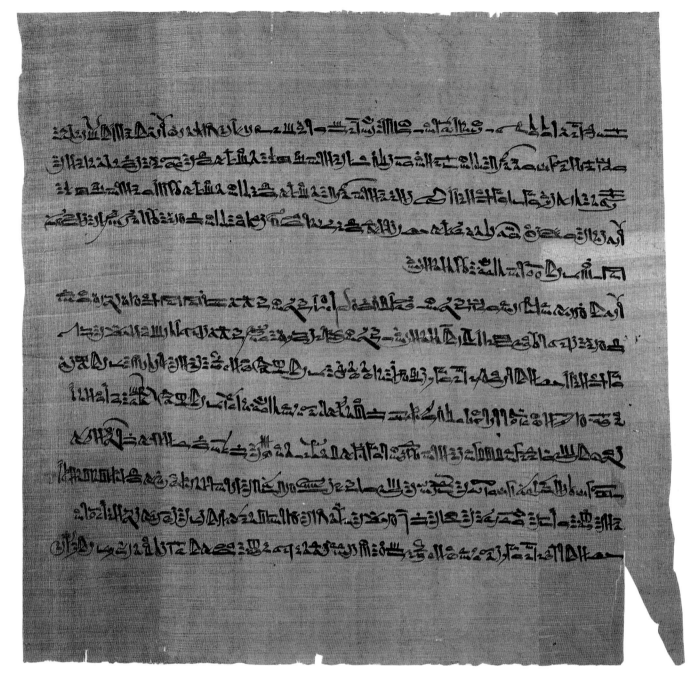

cartouches. He managed to decipher 79 different royal names, of which he recognized and tabulated all the letters one by one. Then, using the 'alphabet', all the letters of which he had progressively recovered, he managed to identify words. In only a couple of years he compiled a dictionary and grammar. Although the readings of kings' names provided the key to the writing system, it would not have led to an understanding of the Egyptian language without the assistance of Coptic. In studying the Rosetta stone text, Champollion's knowledge of Coptic enabled him to work out the phonetic values of particular hieroglyphic signs while his understanding of the Greek text helped him to identify the pictorial characters.

With a knowledge of the language we are now able to translate the countless ancient writings that have survived. The wisdom texts were the most highly regarded and oldest writings, and were popular throughout Egyptian history. They often contain moral codes and represent a high level of thinking. Besides religious literature and business records the Ancient Egyptian writings include subjects as varied as poetry, medicine and mathematics.

ABOVE: *The hieratic script in a particularly fine hand from 'The Great Harris Papyrus', the longest papyrus known. (British Museum.)*

ABOVE RIGHT: *The papyrus of the scribe Ani, one of the finest examples of the Egyptian Book of the Dead. (British Museum.)*

RIGHT: *Painted hieroglyphs on a Middle Kingdom coffin. (British Museum.)*

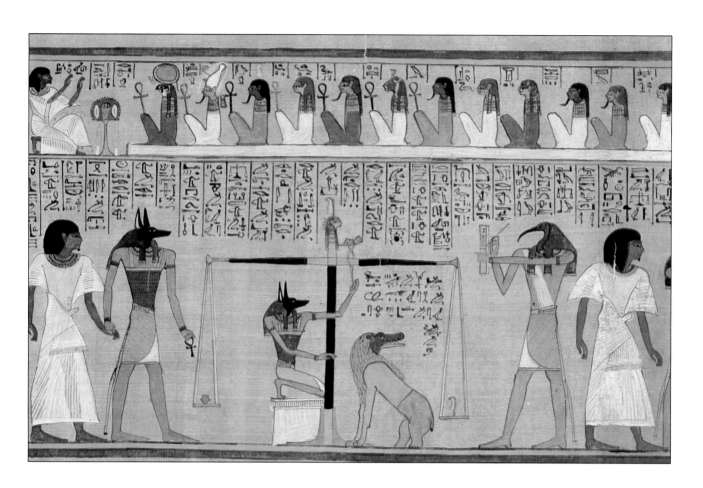

CHAPTER NINE

The INFLUENCE *of* ANCIENT EGYPT

ABOVE: Alethe –
Priestess of Isis *by Edwin
Lond (1829–91). Such
19th-century oil paintings
reflect an idealistic romantic
image of Ancient Egypt.*

The impressive monuments and fascinating artefacts are today's visible evidence of Egypt's past glory. However, many invisible aspects of our modern civilization have their origins in Ancient Egypt. Their ideas were spread to Europe via the Greeks and the Romans, whose own culture drew heavily on this legacy, and who were impressed by the achievements of a civilization so much older than their own. Ancient Egypt has become increasingly distant, mysterious and fascinating ever since. It has also become a potent vehicle for escapism which has inspired art, novels, crime fiction, science fiction, epic and horror movies. In addition many people develop a quest to discover some hidden or secret knowledge in Ancient Egypt and devise complex theories on the construction and purpose of the pyramids. The Ancient Egyptians themselves never went out of their way to spread their culture and religion to the rest of the world, and their influence took place by force of circumstance.

Trade helped to spread Egyptian culture throughout the ancient world. The Egyptians needed wood, metals, and semi-precious stones while their monopoly on African products, particularly gold, attracted countless foreigners. Ideas and technical knowledge travelled with produce. Cultural interchange between Africa, Asia and the Mediterranean countries increased during certain periods of invasion and conquest. The Phoenicians, who were sea-faring traders, borrowed and adapted many Egyptian architectural and artistic elements and spread them throughout the Mediterranean to mainland Greece.

The early Greek writers who travelled to Egypt themselves acknowledged the influence of Egypt on Greek principles of architecture and geometry. The earliest, archaic Greek sculpture reflects both the pose (with the left foot forward) and the proportions of that of Egypt. Before Socrates, followers of Pythagoras came to Egypt to complete their studies of geometry, astronomy and theology, and Egyptian story-telling was also an important influence on the development of the Hellenistic novel. In addition, some aspects of Ancient Greek religion can be traced to Egypt. The Greeks were also inspired by Egyptian medical science, and Egyptian doctors were employed by the Hittites and the Persians.

Scholars have attempted to demonstrate the development of our alphabet from hiero-

glyphic signs, and certain concepts of Egyptian law may also have come down to us. However, perhaps the greatest Ancient Egyptian legacy has been their calendar which was adopted by the Romans and formed the basis of our Gregorian calendar.

The Romans, like the Greeks before them, absorbed many native religious beliefs after they conquered Egypt. They adopted Egyptian burial practices, developing a sophisticated embalming technique and style of funerary portraiture. Many Egyptian gods were also

ABOVE: Israel in Egypt *by Sir Edward Poynter (1836–1919).*

BELOW: The Finding of Moses *by Sir Lawrence Alma Tadema (1836–1912). Biblical subjects provided artists with an excuse for indulging in fanciful visions of Ancient Egypt.*

worshipped although their true nature was often totally misunderstood. The Romans imported many Egyptian statues and made many, often spurious, copies of them. Obelisks stood in the Temple of Isis and in the circuses in Rome. Since Rome became the most important city in the Classical and Christian world, the Roman selection and interpretation of Egyptian forms strongly influenced the way the rest of Europe viewed Ancient Egypt. Consequently, the knowledge handed down to Medieval and Renaissance

Europe was largely governed by what interested classical and Byzantine scholars.

The Bible has provided the only point of access to Ancient Egypt for many Christians over the centuries and it is inevitably coloured by certain prejudices. The Old Testament gives a general impression of the Egyptians as a powerful pagan state oppressing a weaker and devout nomadic people. The Jews like many nomadic people were attracted to Egypt's land of plenty and when they left they must have taken with them many native Egyptian ideas. Egyptian hymns and wisdom literature were known in Canaan from the time of the New Kingdom, and they influenced certain Old Testament writings. Meanwhile, Solomon may well have been inspired by the efficiency of Egyptian bureaucracy when organizing the Jewish kingdom.

It is often demonstrated that Christian religion contains many practices and images which had their roots in pagan Egypt. This is quite understandable since during the formative years of Christianity, the religious rituals inherited from the Romans were already steeped in Egyptian traditions. When the powerful Roman Empire officially adopted

ABOVE: Sandstorm in the Desert *by David Roberts (1796–1864), who visited Egypt in 1839. He sketched many monuments and his drawings were published in a famous series of lithographs.*

BELOW: *Bronze figure of the god Horus as a Roman soldier. The Romans adapted many Egyptian gods into their own culture without fully understanding their original religious function. (British Museum.)*

RIGHT: *The well-preserved mummy of Ramses III, which has provided the model for many horror films.*

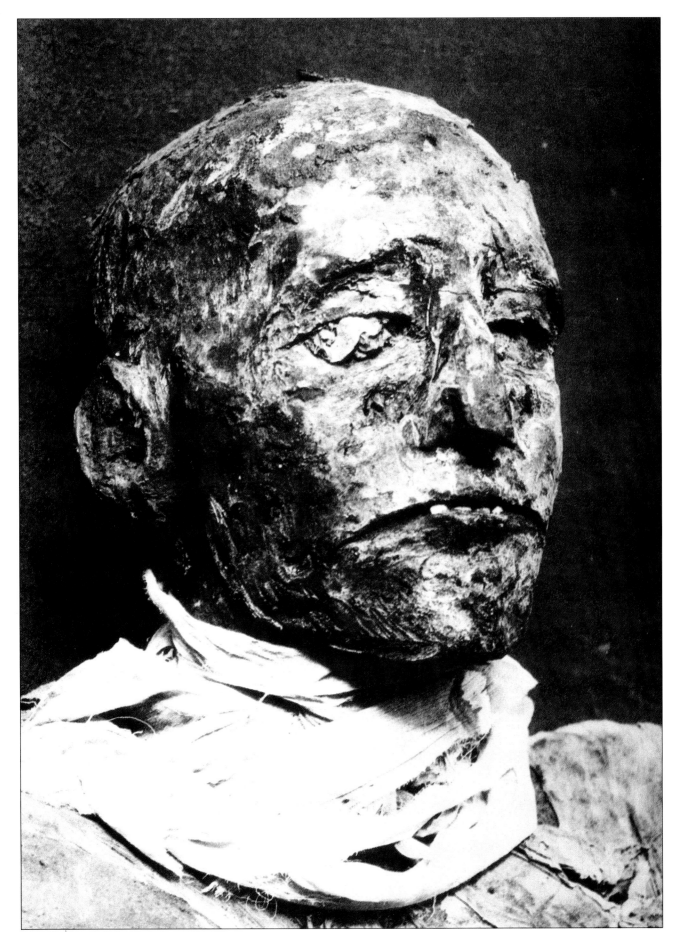

LEFT: *Painted fresco in a Coptic Church. The early Christian Church in Egypt borrowed many elements from the ancient 'pagan' heritage and the Ancient Egyptian language is still spoken today during the services.*

RIGHT: *Mummy of a Roman boy. The Romans adopted the native Egyptian burial customs and added naturalistic portraits to them. (British Museum.)*

FAR RIGHT: *19th-century painted bronze candlestick in the Egyptian style.*

the new Christian religion it embraced many existing concepts and images. In particular, the cult of Isis, so strong in the early Roman Empire, could have provided a prototype image of the Virgin and Child through the many representations of Isis suckling Horus. It is recorded that an original ancient statue of Isis survived in a French church until the sixteenth century, while in a different French church the birth of Isis continues to be celebrated nowadays. The popular representation of Christ triumphant over harmful beasts bears a striking resemblance to the image of Horus triumphant over the crocodile. Many similar parallels can be drawn between the portrayal of certain Christian saints and Egyptian gods while holy attributes like the halo, crook and the idea of winged men as angels have Egyptian precedents. The central Christian emblem, the cross, is often represented on early Coptic monuments as the Egyptian Ankh sign of life and is still clearly present on medieval tomb stones in the Balkans. Many subconscious Egyptian elements would have been conveyed by the bishops from Egypt who were highly influential at the early church councils in Rome.

Egyptian literature also influenced many famous Eastern folklore tales like Sinbad and Ali Baba, while many ancient phrases and sayings probably survive in modern Egypt and the rest of Africa. Certain Ancient Egyptian techniques and ritual practices have survived among the central African peoples,

probably via the later Ethiopian kingdom of Meroe. In modern Egypt, although the influence of Islamic culture has been considerable, many age-old customs have survived. In the countryside, the Shaduf is still used to water the fields, as depicted in ancient times, and many aspects of village life have change little. Some boundaries have altered little and certain ancient place names have remained virtually the same. At Luxor a sacred barque is carried in honour of an Islamic saint very much as it would have been for the god Amun in ancient times. Many superstitions have also survived, such as leaving food or burning incense for dead relatives. There is also a fear of the 'evil eye', and charms are still kept as protection against evil.

Ancient Egypt has continued to be a source of inspiration for mystics and followers of the occult. The hermetic creed, alchemy and astrology probably originated from Alexan-

dria which became a major cultural and trading centre in the ancient world. It was here that many Ancient Egyptian, Greek and Near Eastern ideas and beliefs merged together. Hermetic writings popularized the notion that Egyptians possessed true and pure wisdom. Although astrology arrived late in Egyptian history, probably from Western Asia, there are many depictions of stars, constellations and maps of the sky which have been mistaken for true zodiacs by mystics. The Egyptians did have a system of determining lucky and unlucky influences of the day, as in modern daily horoscopes, which however, had no connection with the 12 signs of the zodiac. The lucky or unlucky character of the day was derived from mythological events which had taken place on these particular days. In Egyptian literature there was also a belief that certain numbers had a magical significance, and this may have found its way into our modern superstition for lucky and unlucky numbers.

The earliest tale about a magician is in the 'Westcar' papyrus which dates from *c*1700 BC, and many psychics, fortune-tellers and palmists call themselves by Egyptian names or claim to be reincarnated Egyptian priests

ABOVE: 19th-century porcelain plate decorated with lotus flowers in the Egyptian style.

RIGHT: Feeding the Sacred Ibis Birds in the Halls of Karnak by Sir Edward Poynter (1836–1919). Such engravings popularized the Egyptian style.

or priestesses. The strange animal-headed gods, mysterious hieroglyphic writing, sacred amulets and funerary beliefs of the Ancient Egyptians provide excellent subject matter for clairvoyants and psychic writers. It is even rumoured that they sell genuine powdered mummy in a New York pharmacy for use in occult magic potions.

The Ancient Egyptian influence on the occult is reinforced by many tales of the 'mummy's curse' which continue to capture public imagination. The earliest record of a ghost story involving a mummy was written in France in 1699. 'The Mummy' together with 'Dracula' and 'Frankenstein' prove that the theme has remained ever-popular for horror movies. Ancient Egypt's connection with the occult was publicized when the so-called 'Curse of Tutankhamun' was claimed by the press to be responsible for the death of Lord Carnarvon. Carnarvon, the expedition's sponsor who had a history of ill-health, died from an infected mosquito bite shortly after the tomb's discovery. However, those wishing to support the superstition about his death never pointed out that the man mainly responsible for the famous find, Howard Carter, lived until well into his sixties. *The*

THE INFLUENCE OF ANCIENT EGYPT

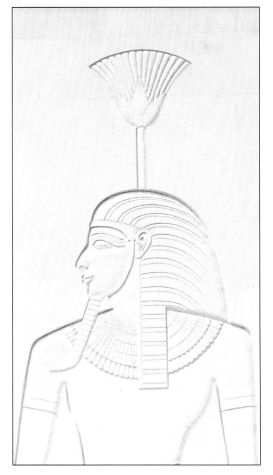

ABOVE: *Silver salt dish, c 1840s, decorated in the Egyptian Revival style.*

LEFT: *Colossal bas-relief from a modern DIY centre building in Kensington, London, which reflects the vogue for Egyptian revival architecture in the 1990s.*

FACING PAGE:

The Egyptian House, Penzance. Built in the 1830s, this structure represents the Egyptian Revival style in architecture.

Times had been granted the exclusive reporting rights on the tomb's discovery, and its rival newspapers, having no story to report, were forced to invent one. This was how the mythical 'curse' was born.

In addition to influencing the occult sciences, Ancient Egypt has continued to inspire Western art through its exotic and romantic associations. In the nineteenth century a number of European painters succeeded in producing some highly imaginative reconstructions of Ancient Egypt. This was in response to a general taste for Middle-Eastern subjects at the time, and many artists travelled all over the Islamic world. The subject matter of their paintings inevitably included turbanned Arabs, bustling bazaars, camels, palm-trees and mildly pornographic harem scenes. The pyramids and the ancient ruins of Egypt were part of this romantic ideal and are often depicted in exaggerated perspective with dramatic sunsets. These elements of the fantastic, exotic and erotic were part of many artists' fanciful visions of Ancient Egypt. Their remarkable attention to detail was a reflection of contemporary Orientalist and Pre-Raphaelite ideals. Many artists must have visited museums in order to make accurate

ABOVE: *Sphinx car mascot from a 1920s car reflects the popularity of Egyptian motifs following the discovery of Tutankhamun's tomb.*

LEFT: *Verdi's epic opera* Aida *continues to be staged as a lavish spectacle and perpetuates the myth of Egypt's ancient splendour.*

often called the 'Egyptian Revival' and it was popular in France and England throughout the Napoleonic War, with its Egyptian connection. However, the Egyptian elements were stylized to suit contemporary taste, and the figures took on a rounder, plumper style reminiscent of the Ancient Graeco-Roman Egyptian style. 'Egyptianizing' was also a feature of English and French furniture of the Regency and Empire periods and was applied to other items like clocks, candelabra and porcelain. This mixture of Egyptian and Classical forms was also used in buildings as varied as mills, law-courts, masonic lodges and cemeteries. By the 1850s, the inclusion of an Egyptian court in the Great Exhibition in London showed that Ancient Egypt had captured British public imagination, reflecting the Victorian taste for ornament and decoration.

In the twentieth century, the artistic interpretation of Ancient Egypt has become less cluttered and elaborate and more 'modern'. The lofty, spacious and geometric character of Egyptian forms are more in tune with modern taste than the Classical style. The discovery of Tutankhamun's tomb in the 1920s was a major influence of a new design movement called Art Deco. Many Egyptian forms were stylized and incorporated into contemporary architecture, furniture, sculpture and graphic art. Ancient Egypt also had a big influence on the newly formed movie industry which was generated from Hollywood. The design of many cinema façades was inspired by Egyptian temple architecture and helped to enhance the whole fantasy world of movies. Meanwhile, Ancient Egyptian themes provided the perfect vehicle for escapist epics like *Land of the Pharaohs*, *The Ten Commandments* and *Cleopatra* which had huge sets with casts of thousands. This grand vision of Egypt's ancient splendour is similarly captured in the world of opera by Verdi's spectacular *Aida*.

Modern artists continue to be inspired by Ancient Egypt and highly original talents like Pablo Picasso and Henry Moore both acknowledged its influence on their formative work. In recent years architects have taken a renewed interest in Egypt and forms such as the pyramid, continue to be stylishly applied to many public and commercial buildings. The Egyptian style is so ancient that it appears modern, and as we progress into the future, so does our knowledge of civilized man's most distant past become more relevant.

studies of original ancient artefacts. The Bible also provided Ancient Egyptian themes for paintings which are frequently charged with considerable sentiment and melodrama. Many of these images became popularized through engravings in contemporary family Bibles and children's scripture books.

For the decorative arts and architecture, Ancient Egyptian motifs provided a variation on the fashionable neo-Classical style. This is

LEFT: *A Greek period bronze statuette of the god Amen Ra shows how Egyptian forms were misrepresented by later cultures. (British Museum.)*

INDEX

Italic numerals refer to illustrations or their captions

PICTURE CREDITS
and
ACKNOWLEDGEMENTS

The author wishes to thank his colleagues at the British Museum for their assistance and encouragement, particularly Dr Stephen Quirke; also Peter Daniel for his invaluable contribution to the photography in this book.

t = top; b = bottom; l = left; r = right.

¶ The Bridgeman Art Library: pages 99 t, 99 b. ¶ Courtesy of the British Museum: pages 54 tl, 55 tl, 56, 61 t, 63. ¶ Peter Daniel: pages 21 t, 21 b, 25, 27, 28t, 28 b, 30, 34 t, 34 b, 35 t, 35 b, 41 tl, 41 tr, 41 br, 42 l, 43 r, 44, 48 tl, 48 tr, 49 t, 49 b, 51 tl, 51 tr, 51 bl, 52 l, 53 tl, 53 tr, 53 br, 54 tr, 57 b, 58 t, 58 b, 59, 60, 61 b, 62 tl, 64, 66, 67 tl, 67 tr, 68 b, 68 tl, 69 t, 69 bl, 69 br, 70 t, 72, 73 t, 73 b, 74 t, 75 l, 76, 77 t, 77 b, 78 centre, 79 centre, 79 b, 80 r, 81 b, 83 t, 83 b, 86, 87, 90 l, 90 r, 91 t, 91 b, 93, 95 l, 95 r, 96, 97, 100 b, 102 r, 103, 104, 105, 107 t, 108 t, 109. ¶ Nina Davies: pages 78 t, 79 t, 80 t, 80 l, 84, 95 t. ¶ Werner Forman Archive: pages 37, 40, 45. ¶ Kevin Jacobsen Promotions: page 108 b. ¶ Richard Kindersley: page 107 b. ¶ James Putnam: pages 26, 32, 39 l, 39 r, 46 t, 82, 85, 94. ¶ Russell-Cotes Art Gallery, Bournemouth: page 98. ¶ Dr Simon Stoddart/ David Dunlop: page 18.

DEDICATION
TO MY FATHER, C. S. PUTNAM